A Leap to an Ecological Economy

Fourth edition

Comments sent to the author on earlier editions:

I have read your book and... it remains the book I would have liked to have written... You have described a way forward... Thank you for your important contribution to the literature in the field of ecological economics.

Glenn Griffin MD, MSc, MEd

Convinced the present... economic system can't help us survive imminent collapse from... the climate crisis, Derek Paul sets out a new hopeful ecological economics, based on the life principle, the recognition that all life... is interconnected and dependent on Earth for survival. Paul's ecological economics would replace the present economy of waste with a sustainable system. In a well-organized text with succinct chapters and useful scholarly references, he aims to promote discussion at both community and policy-making levels.

Phyllis Creighton (historian, editor)

... Naming the major elements that have to shift..., and the key steps to make the shift, moves the debate beyond... the end of oil into the emergent shape of the new paradigm... my deep appreciation for your work...

Bob Fugere, NGO director

Bravo for an extraordinary effort to see things right. The book is both modest and immoderately visionary... yet it covers a vast expanse without coming across as superficial. On the contrary you have done and summarized a great amount of diligence in addressing a subject of truly immense scope and complexity.

Franklyn Griffiths, Prof Emeritus, Political Science

The aim of this book is certainly essential, and I find myself in agreement with all the major topics expressed and explained in the 22 chapters... I certainly will pass the book along to friends to learn ... the important message expressed so succinctly here.

J. Hellebust, biologist

# A Leap to an Ecological Economy

## Derek Paul

Maison Hilton    fourth edition

Date of publication: August 2023

Catalogue information
ISBN   **978-1-7751498-7-3**

Type: non-fiction: economics, paradigm change. capital, investment, resources, employment, how to increase natural wealth, industry, recycling, advertising, benefit corporations, the commons, population, farming, health, militarism, inequality, economic indices.

BISAC category: BUS072000  **BUSINESS & ECONOMICS** / Development/ Sustainable Development

# Contents

# Acknowledgments

My sincere thanks go to Lee Soderstrom, and Sam Lanfranco, whose comments and help were the keys to necessary change in this new edition.

My repeated thanks go out to those who had contributed to this book's previous editions: Robert Hoffman (since deceased), Adam Newns, David Millar, Matthew Kiernan, Don Chisolm, Don Hudson, Paul Prechner, Robert Fugere, Phyllis Creighton, Louis Robichaud, Ortiz Cabrera, Frank Feather, Metta Spencer, Adele Buckley, Adrian Kuzminski, Yves Bergeron, Ted Mann, Sheila Murray, and Robert Murray (since deceased), Cymri Gomery, Sam Lanfranco, and Matthew Chapman and, above all, Lilya Prim-Chorney. Much of their useful comment is still clearly visible. My thanks go also to Sylvie Rochette for encouragement and new contacts and to Mathis Wackernagel for support and help.

# Author's Preface to the fourth edition

Dear reader,

Your role in the matter of establishing a new kind of economy is more important than you can perhaps imagine as you read these pages. Sure, the chapters may each tell you something useful, but nobody yet knows how to put the whole together, into a workable system. This is because of the immense complexity of any system in a technological age, coupled with the formidable opposition to any important change in a world where everyone has been taught that money and profit are the important elements one needs to attend to in order to survive.

The problem is that we humans have been living far too extravagantly, and that we have tended to ignore this for the convenience and comfort that modern production was giving us. In or about 1969, the global population began to "spend" more than it could afford of its resources and or to pollute more than the planet could absorb. This fact was not known prior to the development of the concept of ecological footprint, which was introduced in 1992, and years of work were needed before a global footprint network could supply reliable information.

For the last twenty or more years, however, we have had no excuse for continuing the extravagance and waste. We have also learned that the extravagances of the richer countries were already large in 1969, while many underdeveloped countries used relatively small amounts of resources.

Worse still, the use of coal and oil products is particularly polluting; and burning these resources created the climate threat.

We humans therefore find ourselves needing to live far less extravagantly and to refrain from burning anything that puts carbon dioxide into the atmosphere, and to make these changes quickly and effectively.

Clearly, such a difficult challenge requires the highest measure of international cooperation.

We live in a crowded world, in which the supply of food for eight billion people needs to be grown and distributed—a major challenge even in a world at peace. Enter war, into this picture. In its mildest form it is already in total opposition to all the objectives mentioned above.

We are all in this together. There is much to do.

# Chapter One

## Introduction

The purpose of this book is to outline the fundamental changes in economics that are needed to bring the human race through its present series of crises. The most serious of the crises is long-term—namely, climate change. And it needs to be addressed now, because it is urgent (see Appendix 1) and people and governments have ignored the threat or set it aside for far too long. Numerous economists and other scholars have gradually recognized that climate change cannot be addressed within the traditional economy and, because of the urgency, it is vital to change economic thinking and practices. Because I want to develop the thread of new, ecological economics with a minimum of digression, the important subjects of climate change and other factors threatening humanity are to be found in Appendices.

The most important of the needed economic changes will lie deep in the minds of individuals everywhere—a change of paradigm. The word *paradigm* is often used loosely nowadays, to mean merely an idea or concept. But a paradigm is much more; it refers to a system of thought, and is the hidden skeleton upon which that system developed. Most people are not even aware of that skeleton, because they learned the system of thought within their family, and through contact with friends and teachers, and other influences including the media. Nobody ever mentions the origins of that thinking. The classical paradigm, the framework that led to economic thinking beginning in seventeenth-century Europe, is behind the development of the traditional economic system, as it operates today. It was not present everywhere in the world, but spread to increasing numbers of cultures as they acquired modern industry and the ideas that go with it. It will not be possible to change the economic system without changing the paradigm that underlies it, so we must look at the classical paradigm and also its needed replacement. A colleague of mine and I recently rewrote our paper on exactly this theme [1].

The following are the beliefs the classical paradigm rested upon [2]: we must be rational and reject superstition;

humankind, being distinct from and superior to animals, has been given "dominion over" Nature and has the right and duty to control it;

growth (of industry, civilization etc.) is good *per se*, including human population growth;

technological progress is good *per se*.

In the new paradigm, only the demand for rationality remains from the old one, and at its center is the need to respect the Earth and sustain all of life in its fullness of diversity [1]. The new paradigm thus recognizes the interdependence of species, of which we humans are only one among very many. And here lies the clash between the old and the proposed new economics. While traditional economics allows us to exterminate cod, wolves and bees, and to pump steers full of growth hormones, the new paradigm requires respect for life, and so must the new economics. Today's protesters against extermination are part of the avant-garde in new thinking.

The new paradigm isn't really new, since the indigenous peoples have generally evolved to respect the Earth and its species, and many people even in Western civilization have also done so; but these latter were not the drivers of the economic system.

The change in paradigm and therefore of attitude is now brought upon us by necessity because, if we don't change, we are done for. Some of the indigenous sages of America have seen the collapse of Western civilization as inevitable, while Canadian author Ronald Wright called the traditional economy a suicide machine [3].

Readers who have read the essay, "The Essential Paradigm Shift" [1] will have noted the element of feminism within it, which, from the author's viewpoint, speaks of reviving the social equality between women and men that had existed in old Europe prior to 4300 B.C. [4]. The most recent evidence of that equality comes from the society of ancient Crete, which managed to avoid the take-over of Europe by male dominant, warring societies until c.1500 B.C., when Crete fell to Greece. Crete had, however, suffered two previous invasions in which the victors discovered that Cretan civilization was preferable to their own, and adopted Cretan ways. Adopting the new paradigm cannot abolish the memory of appalling wars, but it can produce a mentality that sets war aside permanently, together with its weaponry. Today warfare anywhere is preventing us from addressing climate change and impedes the development of a sustainable economy.

The last three centuries have seen the economy in a state of evolution, with the adjective *neoliberal* applying to the phase since about 1980 when banking was much deregulated. This book is not an attempt to reverse the trends of the last 30 or more years, but to replace the entire gamut of variants of the economy that derived from the classical paradigm. I needed a word to describe these collectively, and chose *traditional*. But the word *neoliberal* will appear on these pages, especially when meaning the excesses of these last years. Another common expression nowadays is *regenerative economy*, meaning a new type of economy that respects the Earth and its creatures. Why did I therefore not call this book *A Leap to a Regenerative Economy* back in 2017? At that time I had not seen all of features of a fully ecological economy in the literature on regenerative economy. If the difference has by now disappeared, so much the better.

This book was strongly influenced by the work of the late Hazel Henderson. Her 37-page book, Mapping the Global Transition to the Solar Age (2014) can still be downloaded from the internet.

If this book generates controversy, then at least it will have opened important debates. The text is designed to prompt discussion both at the community and policy-making levels. Getting the best future requires envisioning that future and deriving the pathway from there to here.

## Other threats

Climate change is by no means the only major threat to humanity. Much closer in time are threats such as collapse of civilization, global war, and collapse of individual national economies.

Avoiding a collapse of civilization requires the same prescription as facing up to climate change, which includes a major shift toward international cooperation.

Avoiding war, especially global war also requires a shift to cooperation, and away from confrontation and technological competition (see Chapter Eighteen). National economic failures must, for the time being, be dealt with individually, with understanding, generosity and, where possible, avoidance of major displacement of people.


## What follows

Chapter Two outlines the character of traditional economics and why it must be replaced. Chapter Three lists fifteen respects in which an ecological economy must differ from the traditional one. Chapter Four is a primer on money, money creation and debt. Chapter Five explains the centrality of capital in economics and comments on what investment in stocks and shares may be like in an ecological economy as part of the effort to make the economy sustainable. The other sense of the word *investment*, namely, investing so as to increase natural wealth and infrastructure, is dealt with in Chapter Six, which together with Chapters Seven through Twenty outline what must or might be done to bring about a fully ecological economy. Then follow a chapter on China, inserted because of the importance of its economy and its currently enormous greenhouse gas emissions, and a chapter of recommendations.

Many of the notes refer to works written in the language of traditional economics, a thought process I try to avoid. But it is necessary to acknowledge good ideas, even if they emerged from the old thinking.

**Notes**

1. Phyllis Creighton and Derek Paul "The Essential Paradigm Shift" 2020. https://www.derekleverpaul.ca

2. The second and third of these statements are recognizable as biblical in origin. It helps when trying to understand the classical paradigm to recall that, in the days of Isaac Newton, nearly everyone in Christian Western Europe took biblical statements as literally true. Current economics had its roots in that same age, along with the onset of banking. To a good approximation, economics was carried forward by the classical paradigm until today. In these last decades increasingly many people have contributed to steering economics into new directions, recognizing the need for new thinking.

3. Ronald Wright *A Short History of Progress* House of Anansi Press 2004.

4. Marija Gimbutas *The Goddesses and Gods of Old Europe: 6500-3500 B.C., Myth and Cult images* Thames and Hudson 1982. In the conclusions she wrote that the world of myth was not polarized into female and male as it was among the Indo-European and many other nomadic peoples of the steppes. The male and female "principles" were manifest side by side… Neither was subordinate to the other: by complementing one another, their power was doubled.

# Chapter Two
## Why the Traditional System Must Be Replaced

Several of my scientific colleagues recognized long before I did that the present economic system, which I shall call *traditional*, is doomed. The system, which proponents see as a free-enterprise, free-market system in which the chartered banks can create new money, has earned other descriptions in the last forty years such as *neoclassical, neoliberal,* and *neoconservative*. But my colleagues simply called it *capitalism*, and said it must be replaced. Two of them felt that its replacement could only be achieved through violent revolution. I could not accept the notion of neoliberalism's violent overthrow, because the recovery time following such a revolution would exceed the time we have left to establish a sustainable economy and engage in the huge collaborative effort needed to address climate change. Aside from my personal abhorrence of violence and of the moral questions involved, a violent revolution would therefore take too long. Others have argued privately that it is already too late and civilization is doomed, but I reject that view because one of the few certainties about the future is that it will be full of surprises.

Many authors have made cogent cases against our traditional economy declaring it one of waste. Two books on the need for change in the economic system are important here: Speth's *Another America is Possible* [1] and Smith and Max-Neef's *Economics Unmasked* [2]. The latter provides a broad, historical perspective and makes a cast-iron case against the traditional economy and for the need to replace it, while Speth argues against the current form of free-market economy, and all support their points with mountains of evidence. Philip Smith, in his chapters in *Economics Unmasked*, systematically points out how the traditional model contradicts itself and fails to match reality. All three authors base their arguments on justice: what appears to be right and good for people and their natural environment. By contrast, traditional economics as practiced furthers the interests of the rich, and fails to advance the interests of the very numerous poor, whose plight is deemed of no consequence in traditional economic thinking. Were that not so, then the last forty years would have allowed plenty of time for the increasing inequalities in developed countries to be redressed. But the gap between rich and poor gradually increased during these last 45 years. I wrote this book knowing full well that those in control would give little thought to values like justice [3], so I have chosen to emphasize something we can all relate to: the imminent collapse of the system [4].

Many other authors have objected to the present economic system, which authorizes enterprises to pursue profit as if resources were limitless, and as if the Earth could absorb any and all pollution that results from human activities. Therefore accounting has been based on such direct elements as the financial cost of extracting a raw material (without regard to environmental damage done in the process) and the costs of manufacturing, without concern for where the products end up, which could be landfill, lakes, rivers, the ocean, or the atmosphere.

There are many exceptions to the generalities just expressed, and some of these are beautifully recounted by Hazel Henderson [5], but the broad truth remains. When industries behave in the public interest, it is often because of regulation, not innate desire on the part of the corporation. Businesses detest being regulated, as is evidenced by recurring political efforts to bring about deregulation.


**Characteristics of a traditional economy**

To facilitate comparison between the traditional economy of today and a fully ecological economy, the paragraphs that follow are labeled as in Chapter Three, which characterizes an ecological economy.

a) The traditional economy fails to **distinguish between money and wealth**, and measures wealth in terms of money. This follows from the assumption that money can buy anything, while ignoring that a desired good may have a value unrelated to money. There are also forms of wealth, like wellbeing, that are not measurable in terms of money.

b) The traditional economy depends upon cheap labor to maximize profit. It is easier to obtain labor when there is a shortage of available employment. At the same time, businesses can best sell their products when people can afford to buy them, that is, when employment is at a maximum. The compromise is a society enjoying moderately high employment, for example, one in which four to seven percent of the working population is seeking work. In times of recession, however, which are all too frequent and cause great hardship, employment drops radically. By contrast, full employment is rarely even talked about. I define it here as a situation in which all those who are able to work and who are seeking employment can at least find something. I hold that full employment is practicable, desirable, and essential for an ecological economy (see Chapter Seven). The traditional economic system has no built-in method of dealing with recessions, so the people depend on outside interference, usually government action. For example, governments might inject new money into the system to get factories back into production, and make businesses profitable again. However, such a strategy makes no sense when goods have been overproduced. Traditional thinking tends to lead to gross errors, as was seen after the crash in 2008. Following that recession very large sums of new money were created several times in the USA to stimulate the economy, but very much of the money found its way into the "tertiary" (that is, non-productive) part of the economy [6]. Thus a financial injection can put money primarily into the pockets of investors. Not nearly enough went into increasing prosperity across the entire U.S. community. There are also historic examples of money creation where communities did benefit. President Roosevelt's *New Deal* in the 1930s may be considered one of them, but it received much opposition from traditional business and economic thinkers.

c) The traditional economy disregards negative effects of its chosen pathways, such as basing its energy supply largely on burning fossil fuels, even though the results are extremely harmful to life on Earth. It

16

continues to favor the petroleum industry, including governments rewarding corporations with subsidies, when renewable energy currencies are already available and preferable on important grounds.

d) The traditional economy encourages extraction of primary resources, to maximize yield and industrial throughput, consequently increasing pollution of land, air, and water.

e) Industrial and business practices, though excellent in more and more cases, lag behind what is needed for attaining sustainability, partly because of the legal basis of corporations. Highly undesirable practices include planned obsolescence. The system measures economic success in terms of money instead of quality of life.

f) The traditional system favors globalized markets so as to increase trade and profit without regard for the overall economic benefit as reckoned by including local production and all environmental factors.

g) The legitimate practice of advertising goods and services for sale, has, with the long-term assistance of focused psychological study, enabled the advertising industry to bring a large segment of human society into a state of obsession with consumer goods, sometimes amounting to an addiction to shopping. The evidence is the widespread practice of purchasing goods not needed by the purchasers or their families. Such consumerism sustains the productive economy, but does so at the price of producing excess waste. The economic system ignores real economic and sociological needs.

h) Until 2010, legislation pertaining to the creation of new corporations in almost every jurisdiction held corporations responsible to their shareholders only for making profit. This narrow requirement has had many regrettable consequences, including environmental degradation. In countries where the law tends to be enforced, much can be done through governmental regulation, or through systems of certification. In poor countries, however, where the income provided by royalties on extracted ores can be desperately needed, environmental damage amounts to a loss of natural wealth suffered by the State. A shaft of new light appeared in 2010 with the creation of *benefit corporations* in a good many U.S.

states (see Chapter Thirteen), a welcome departure from the long history of regulation and corporate efforts to achieve deregulation under traditional economics.

i) Chartered banks in "Western" economies occupy positions of considerable privilege, having the right (by arrangement with their national bank) to issue new money at interest, to trade in international currencies, and to run investing businesses. The system is, however, exploitative of many clients, especially those of low income, young people who have debts on student loans, largely because interest rates are based on risk theory [7]. In addition, national banks have not been used to finance important ecological projects.

j) The traditional economy has not yet come to terms fully with the concept of the *global commons* (see Chapter Fifteen). For example, the ocean and the ocean floor are surely part of the global commons, but trawling has been allowed to wreak havoc there. Likewise, ocean fishing has not been regulated to ensure future fish stocks—many millions of people depend on fish for their protein, making abundant fisheries essential.

k) The traditional economy has nothing to say about global population, though population has a proportional effect on almost all crucial issues facing humankind.

l) Businesses in food and agriculture have succeeded in feeding the rapidly expanding numbers of the human race, but this has been accomplished at a huge price. A whole new brand of agriculture has been developed based upon large monocultures of grain fed by chemical fertilizers, and assisted by massive application of chemicals to control pests. More recently, weed killers have been widely applied to prevent weeds from taking soil nutrients that were placed there to feed grain. The side effects of the pesticides are now known to be highly negative (see Chapter Seventeen), and the glyphosate used as a weed killer ha also been shown to be biologically dangerous [8], though some findings against glyphosate continue to be challenged. Food industries have in addition degraded the food value of grain through industrial processes for grinding that remove the essential nutrients, while bread makers use techniques of leavening that fail to convert gluten into useful protein. Studies of vitamins and minerals in vegetables and fruit also indicate decreased food quality resulting from modern farming (see Chapter Seventeen). Many other factors affecting human health, rooted in the established medical profession and its accompanying drug industry, require attention: the separation of modern medicine from parallel professions; the neglect of great value in natural, herbal treatments. An integrative approach combining the best of both worlds, current-official and parallel, would have much to offer.

m) Militarism became a dominant, threatening factor in human life following the arms build-up to WWI and reaching a new pinnacle in 1945 with the explosion of the first three nuclear bombs, two of which were dropped over Japanese cities. From then, militaries could count on huge government support to develop a previously unimaginable range of new weapon systems. The political power of the military-industrial complex is widespread, to the point it can control some policies of universities that receive large military-related research contracts. Militarism, particularly in its latest form, fits well in the traditional economy, as it creates profit, employs many highly trained people, maximizes the throughput of resources, and can ignore the undoubted disadvantages it brings about. These include extraordinary destruction, maiming and killing (mainly civilians), large-scale displacement of people, massive wastage of resources, and the fact that weapons sold abroad can be used in ways the seller would never have approved. All this fits with the form of accountancy employed, which measures everything in terms of money. Anatol Rapoport, a celebrated peace researcher in his day, maintained that "None of the hypothetical aims of an offensive war bear critical scrutiny under contemporary conditions."

n) Traditional economics has enjoyed a period of unchallenged rule since the 1970s, which has given rise to an increasing gap in wealth between rich and poor, and a new class of super-rich (see Chapter Nineteen).

o) The Gross Domestic Product (GDP) has been much criticized as an index for measuring and expressing prosperity, yet it is continually used and quoted, perhaps because of the simplicity of determining it.

## Notes

1. James Gustave Speth *America the Possible: Manifesto for a New Economy* Yale University Press 2012.

2. Phillip Smith and Manfred Max-Neef *Economics Unmasked* Green Books 2011.

3. By contrast, justice is most important for citizens at large, and the struggle for justice is more and more evident from the activities of nongovernmental agencies and individuals. The need for justice could play an important role in bringing about an ecological economy.

4. The collapse could arise from acute shortages of essential goods (Appendix 2), or militarism and war (Chapter 18), or a combination.

5. Hazel Henderson *Mapping the Global Transition to the Solar Age* internet 2014.

6. John Michael Greer *The Wealth of Nature: Economics as if Survival Mattered* New Society Publishers 2011.

7. The principles laid out in Chapter Four for international loans could be applied within a country to individuals.

8. Polly Higgins *Eradicating Ecocide* Shepheard-Walwyn (Publishers) Ltd 2010 Chapter 3.

# Chapter Three

## Characteristics of an Ecological Economic System

An ecological economy will ensure that the use of resources does not impair future prosperity and, in particular, that nonrenewable resources will be preserved through minimizing extraction and maximizing recycling. In addition, the system must respect the Earth's capacities, and the health of the entire ecosphere. The transition from the old to the new economics presents many challenges, the most important being the widespread adoption of the new paradigm, especially by businesses, heads of industry, banking chiefs, and elected or appointed public servants and politicians who will be legislating and changing the rules where needed. Money will go from controlling what we may and may not do, to facilitating what urgently needs to be done. The relevant factors are discussed more fully in turn, in chapters six through twenty. Here is a list of what an ecological economy must feature:

a) a clear distinction between wealth and money, and taking good care to increase wealth; assessment of wealth in terms of resources: natural, built, and human capital; and accounting both nationally and by corporations in these terms

b) consistent full employment

c) an end to fossil-fuel burning, including what is burned in ocean and air transport

d) minimal extraction of primary resources, including trees, by maximizing re-use and recycling

e) the pursuit of ecologically sound goals and practices in business and industry, and in city and regional development

f) a preference for local production, where beneficial; with changes in long-distance trade to match

g) a transformation of the advertising industry

h) more benefit corporations, with a legislative basis for them everywhere and, perhaps, global standardization of their legal basis; and encouragement of other ecologically responsible enterprises

i) publicly-owned banks (or equivalent machinery) in all single-currency areas, for funding what needs to be done in the EE context

j) clearly-defined global commons, with formation and implementation of policies for their restoration or enrichment

k) sound population policies in all regions, with implementation of policy goals

l) increasing organic farming with a view to eliminating pesticides and herbicides for the sake of planetary health and improving food quality and nutrition, and to increase sequestration of $CO_2$; and rationalizing medicine integratively—for the improvement of human health

m) decreasing militarism and increasing international cooperation

n) a progressive reduction of social inequalities

o) new indices including capital wealth indices to replace GDP for assessment of prosperity and human welfare and the good state of the planet.

This slate of items with full justification of the separate points will likely be a work in progress for some time. All of the material from Chapter Six on is preliminary, in that little of this long menu has yet been achieved anywhere, and there is always the need for more good ideas.

# Chapter Four

## Money and Debt

It will be important to have a good grasp of money and how it is created and how, today, government and its national bank endeavor to have the optimum amount of money in circulation to fulfill various requirements of our economy. We need at least to know this in order to begin evaluating what changes could be beneficial in the design of a future, sustainable economy.

In this chapter, we shall be concerned with the government-approved official money used within countries and exchanged between countries. All manner of privately created money is possible, and readers will find a brief discussion of parallel, private, and cryptocurrencies in Chapter Fourteen. We must first understand what the functions of our official money are, how it is created, and why government has an essential role in maintaining its stability.

We use money primarily for our purchases (trade), for discharging debt, and we store it for later use in bank accounts, and it serves as a unit of account. Money can also have symbolic value. In the complex society that most of us live in, the ability to exchange money for another currency is also important. This means that it is desirable that the relative values of different currencies do not change rapidly. Otherwise, those needing to exchange currencies could suffer large losses merely because a currency that they hold drops sharply relative to another that they need. Exchange rates are also influenced by capital flows and government engagement in foreign markets. Stabilizing the value of money and setting rules for its creation are matters for government and law.

In the 19$^{th}$ century and several times in the 20$^{th}$, much of the world used the Gold Standard, whereby the unit of money was equal to a certain mass (quantity) of pure gold. In 1971 the USA ceased basing its standard unit of account (that is, of money) on a given quantity of pure gold, and other countries followed within the next two years. Since then, commodity money, which bases monetary value on a commodity (usually gold), has been replaced by fiat money (dollar bills, coins and numbers in deposit accounts). "Fiat" means "let it be so" and implies that the intrinsic values of materials such as the paper or plastic of banknotes and the metals of coins have no relation to the values written on the banknotes or stamped on the coins. Such money has been deprecatingly referred to as funny money, since it only retains user trust through the efforts of a government, and its banking system, which, however, go to great lengths to preserve the intended use values.

While money is surely necessary in the operations of modern life, it comes with a price, since the supply and distribution of money in our very complex society often determine what happens, such as whether an important program goes ahead. Who controls money and on what terms is therefore vitally important.

## Money and value

The former basing of value on metallic gold, silver and copper arose from their properties: durability, verification through appearance and density measurement, and malleability for stamping coins of any size. As such they represented a standard of value for centuries. There is, however, no absolute standard of value, even though the investment community in our time does its best to maintain asset value by holding a weighted portfolio of national currencies.

One needs furthermore to distinguish between an exchange value (what goods one can obtain for a unit of currency) and a use value (what that quantity of goods is felt to be worth by its owner, or by a potential buyer).

## Money creation and debt

Once government assumes the duty to control money, the next questions are the forms that money will take. The present legal forms of money are bank notes, low-value coins, and deposits in accounts, all accepted as legitimate.

But where did the money come from in the first place? Was it all created by the national banks? Partially, national banks expand the money supply when they buy assets on the open market. New money is, however, mostly created by the chartered banks, enterprises that are owned by shareholders and have a corporate basis much like that of any other corporation. Banks create money when they make a loan. When a bank lends money, it simultaneously creates debt, the amount of the debt being exactly equal to the amount of money loaned. When such a loan is repaid, the debt vanishes too, and the money supply contracts. Note, however, that debts between individuals or an individual and an enterprise do not change the amount of money M (see below), contrary to what occurs when a loan is made by a bank.

The money available to the people of any given country within the Western system can thus be thought of as consisting of deposits in bank accounts and cash that is in circulation, that is, held by individuals as banknotes and small change. The total money in circulation in a single currency area is often called currency, C, to distinguish it from deposits, D. The total of such accessible money we'll call M: clearly,

$$M = C + D$$

The money, M. is the total accessible for the population and businesses of the area concerned: a whole country or a whole single currency area, such as the European Union. The apparent precision implicit in the equation for M is deceiving unless one distinguishes between different sorts of deposits. For example, deposits such as savings accounts are regarded as being less available for spending, while long-term deposits are even less available. Such deposits give rise to the question: is this money readily accessible for keeping the economy going? For this reason, economists have created money categories. M1 includes checking deposits at chartered banks; M2 includes some other bank deposits, including savings deposits. M2+ adds deposits at credit unions and shares in some financial companies. M3 adds fixed-term deposits of firms and chartered banks. More fine detail can be found in texts [1]. The breakdown into M1, M2, etc. is important because the amounts vary considerably, and they represent different degrees of liquidity (accessibilty).

Mankiw and Scarth give an example in which M1 for Canada is about $190 million CAD, while M3 exceeds $970 million and the amount circulation is less than $45 million.

To complete this picture simply, the base money, B, is defined as the money in circulation plus the reserves of the banks, R:

$$B = C + R$$

One needs to think of the reserve as the portion of the Banks' deposits that are not to be lent out in loans, so that they are deposits with the central bank. The fact that R is usually very small compared with D, the deposits, has the effect that loans made by banks can greatly exceed the banks' total deposits, which enables banks to bring about a sufficiency of money in circulation. The complication with this kind of arithmetic arises because different forms of deposits have different liquidity, and hence have unequal availability for economic transactions.

Lastly, a money multiplier, m, is defined by the equation:

$$m = M/B$$

Banks in Canada and the United States today do not have reserve requirements and are not restricted by law in the amounts they can lend, and usually have outstanding loans greatly in excess of their total deposits.

## National banks

Some national banks are owned by the government of their country, as are the Bank of Canada [2] and the Bank of England [3]; others are corporations owned by their shareholders.

The important functions of a national bank are monetary in that it is the bank of the government itself and, in a different way, of all the chartered banks; it is the national money supplier; it determines monetary policy at arms-length from the government. Its functions include maintaining the supply of currency based on monetary policy objectives which is done by choosing the base rate of interest and engaging in open market operations through buying or selling government bonds. Other ideas for withdrawing money from circulation might in future be justified; an example is mentioned in the next section.

The US national bank known as the Federal Reserve (Fed) consists of regional Fed banks governed by an independent Governing Board appointed by the President of the United States, and with restricted shares owned by a selection of private banks [4]. Its complexity distinguishes it from the Bank of England, for example. The potential for it to develop policy according to regions within the United States could be useful in a transition from the traditional economy to one that is eliminating its greenhouse gas emissions and working toward sustainability.

## Times of stress

When the COVID-19 pandemic struck Canada, it soon became clear that thousands of people were reduced to zero income. The federal response in 2020 was to create $58 billion new dollars to support people whose income had dropped to zero or near zero during the COVID-19 outbreak. The new money increased the total money in circulation by 60 percent, playing a yet-to-be-determined role, along with supply line problems, in the past-pandemic inflation. In cases such as this, the Bank of Canada has options. It can raise its interest rate, which discourages borrowing, especially borrowing from banks. It can sell government bonds, which reduces the currency in circulation by the dollar amount of the bonds purchased. A more selective method of taking money from circulation would be to create a tax having a particular social goal, and transfer the tax so collected to the national bank so as to keep it out of circulation [5].

## Limitations of the system

The difficulties experienced in many countries during the years of economic depression, 1929-1938, are well recorded. In the United

States, by no means the hardest hit country in that long depression, unemployment levels reached 25 percent and never went below 9 percent, despite the efforts of President Hoover to bring relief to the unemployed, and President Roosevelt's New Deal, which began after he took office in 1934. After the fall of France in 1940, the USA increased its production of war supplies to assist Great Britain's war effort and unemployment rapidly declined to 2 percent in the USA, which was then not at war.

The wartime experience in Canada and the USA shows the inadequacies of the free-market economic system when confronting a crisis. Market profit calculus ignores the values of the living ecosphere and the costs of unemployment, pollution, and human carelessness. None of these abuses carry a direct price tag in the marketplace. Profits are privatized and costs are foisted onto society.

## Debt burden

Loans give rise to debts of corresponding amounts. Loans make possible all manner of important projects. Debt, however, holds the sword of Damocles over the heads of those who incur such debt. All loans are subject to the risk that the borrower will be unable to repay. There may be no perfect solution to the dilemma of the burden brought about by unsustainable debt. The history of the Depression (1929-1938) suggests that huge numbers of people were financially ruined by misfortune during those years due to the system having truly major flaws.

A major critique of debt arose again after WWII, when some poor countries could no longer repay international loans that had been negotiated by international financial organizations for their development. In many cases such countries had already repaid amounts exceeding the total borrowed. Some such loans were "forgiven," but this didn't help the countries whose loans were not forgiven. Other unfair debt burden exists to this day, including credit card debt and interest on student loans. I chose the word "unfair" because, in many cases, the debtors who repay their debts are unwittingly repaying at interest rates that cover the money owed by those who defaulted. This problem needs attention to prepare the road toward a sustainable economy.

Public debate is needed on alternative systems for dealing with debt. Not only are interest rates relevant, but also the total amount repayable. Should there be a limit on the total amount to be repaid? How does one combine all factors to reach just solutions for lender and borrower? These are not new questions but are nevertheless unsolved problems.

Debt and interest rates have been very extensively discussed within the traditional economy. The trends within the economy for the last 35 or more years have led to cumulatively increasing debts of governments in the developed world as well as of individuals: and have given rise to crises in several spectacular cases. One example will suffice. The national debts in Europe increased dramatically on average since the formation of the European Union, most critically in the poorer countries. A major factor was the agreement at the time of foundation of the Union that governments would not be permitted to borrow at low interest from their central bank, but only from the chartered banks whose interest rates were significantly higher than that of the central banks. The picture of how Western governments have allowed themselves to get into debt, and now must generate huge budget surpluses just to pay the interest, has been clearly and succinctly described by Louis Gill [6].

A reason the poorest countries were hardest hit in the European Union is the E.U. created a Union wide monetary authority but did not create a coordinated fiscal policy process to deal with regional inequity problems.

**Principles in New Economics**

In 1999 I presented a paper at the international World Order Conference at Ryerson University (now Metropolitan University) in Toronto. In search of a superordinate principle, I coined "The Principle of Life." This implied that adoption of the new paradigm (see Chapter One), based upon taking planetary life as a value, amounts to a superordinate principle, from which very many sub-principles can be derived. For example, all the 26 ecological principles emerging from the U.N.'s Declaration on the Human Environment (1972) are sub-principles of this central principle. The *Golden Rule*, that is, the idea that one should treat others as we would like them to treat us, is also a subprinciple of this very general principle. So is the extension of the Golden Rule from individuals to groups and nations. The United Nations itself is the first manifestation of its extension to the global level. When it comes to economics and money, some sub-principles are easily derived:

1. Loans, especially to poor people or poor countries, must be made on terms that render them repayable without unacceptable social cost. That would imply that some such loans would have to be made at nominal interest by national banks.

2. It is not the business of any lending agency to determine the social policy in a borrower country, though advice in some cases could be valuable.

## Money in an ecological economy

Let's now look at an ecological economy, one in which we address the emergency of climate change. It will be necessary to make money available for many projects at nominal (meaning negligible) interest. The idea of interest-free loans of new money isn't new. It was used by Canadian Prime Minister Mackenzie King to finance Canada's role in WWII. He just asked the Bank of Canada to provide the funds as needed. At the end of the war, the debt was large, but the debt burden was small. There are chartered banks that offer interest-free loans today [7], but not necessarily on the scale that will be required in the future economy.

The projects referred to above will include long-term efforts to restore the fertility of land and go beyond restoration to improvement. It will therefore be important to have ecologists within the organization making the loans who can clearly identify what measures are necessary, so that such vital matters receive priority.

Financing major projects on the scale that will be necessary can cause major inflation. In Britain, during WWII, inflation was held to zero by freezing wages and rents of unfurnished accommodation, and raising taxes on the richer taxpayers. Full employment was also a feature of the economy of WWII. But the analogy between WWII conditions and what is now needed ends there, since the war was essentially destructive, while the ecological economy is essentially constructive and life-giving. In WWII, though the net incomes of the rich were much reduced, the stores carried many fewer goods, rendering the reduced net incomes less difficult to accept. Bringing about an ecological economy with full employment can surely be achieved in the now-prosperous countries without any of the 50 percent poorest individuals becoming poorer. But optimum cooperation of the very rich with national governments will surely be needed. Addressing climate change can only be successful if the population is in agreement with the necessary policies. It is therefore essential not to drive anyone into poverty, and to have everyone involved in the policy discussions.

This discussion is continued in Chapter 14.


**Banking structure and interest rates in an ecological economy**

This is untrodden ground, so let's make a start. The following choices might be used to begin the debate:

- Expand national bank responsibilities beyond dealing with inflation and unemployment, to include funding for ecological projects developed and approved within a new national governance policy process.

- Enable regional banks to fund the local initiatives that come from the national policy process.

- Develop multi-stakeholder policy-making processes where expertise and societal engagement produce ecologically sound policies to be funded by the national bank process.

- Create a multi-stakeholder consultative process, based on The Principle of Life, such as could fuel a rebirth of concern and effort for a sustainable ecological future.

**Notes**

1. N Gregory Mankiw and William Scarth *Macro Economics* third Canadian edition Worth Publishers 2008.

2. For information about the functioning of the Bank of Canada see: https://www.bankofcanada.ca/markets/market-operations-liquidity-provision/

3. The Bank of England claims as its mission: "Promoting the good of the people of the United Kingdom." www.bankofengland.co.uk

4. Several useful articles on the U.S. federal reserve system are available on the Internet.

5. This. idea may be new and is suggested following the work of John Michael Greer on the "third economy" in his book, *The Wealth of Nature: Economics as if Survival Mattered* New Society Publishers 2011 pp.59-68.

6. Louis Gill "Les dettes souveraines et la domination des marchés financiers" ("Sovereign debts and the dominance of financial markets") in *Sortir de l'économie du désastre* eds Bernard Elie et Claude Vaillantcourt *M*éditeur 2012 pp. 77-89.

7. Examples are the JAK Bank in Sweden and the Islamic banks worldwide, notably in Dubai and Pakistan, where the largest is the Meezan Islamic Bank.

# Chapter Five
## Capital and Investment

The failure of almost everyone alive to distinguish between money and wealth is understandable. The human race has lived for over 300 years with an economic system and a banking system that blur the distinction, because it has been assumed all that time that money could buy anything if you had enough of it. Moreover, this was usually the case. However, money cannot buy anything that is simply unavailable, no matter what that something is. After large-diameter tree trunks have all been cut down and used industrially, money will not buy you any more, though you may take steps to ensure a supply some eighty years ahead. Traditional economists continue to support their obsolete system by saying, "Well, if there isn't enough wood, we'll, find a substitute material." [1] This applied across the board (pun intended) to whatever resource is becoming scarce. For example, a response to freshwater shortage is to desalinate the ocean locally and pump the newly produced fresh water to where it is needed. Both processes are energy intensive, and desalination is usually polluting in one or more ways, implying that some other resource is being degraded. The degradation of the biosphere through any such polluting process represents a loss of wealth, but accountants within the traditional system are not obliged to compute such effects or present them in their balance sheets. The accounting is done in terms of money, while the incidental losses of wealth, often of natural wealth, are overlooked no matter how large they are.

A major problem facing the human race is therefore to relearn the important difference between money and wealth, which will bring with it the understanding that one must measure wealth in natural units, even though fiscal accountancy will continue to be a requirement. The National Roundtable on The Environment and the Economy (NRTEE) did Canadians a great service at the end of the last millennium when it produced a set of wealth indices for the federal Department of Finance

[2]. The government hoped thereby to be warned when a natural resource was declining dangerously. No doubt this was prompted by the shock of the collapse in ocean cod stocks late in the 20<sup>th</sup> century. For a time it looked as if that important resource would disappear entirely, and the Finance Department thought that indices might give useful future warnings. NRTEE produced the desired system of indices, and all of them were given in natural units, such as estimated numbers (or tonnages or volume) of fish, lumber, etc.

As part of its work on these indices, NRTEE recognized three types of capital: natural, built, and human. The natural capital was mostly what their index system addressed. Built capital meant wealth that the human race constructs, such as buildings and bridges, objects that have a certain permanence. Human capital is designed to measure the usefulness to human society of its own people, through education and training and their overall capabilities. One can put dollar values on any of these things, but they don't mean much, as they could vary tremendously from day to day, whereas a building that will house six families will presumably have the same value to its users and to society as a whole from one year to the next in the absence of disaster, and provided there is good maintenance.

These notions of capital are fundamental and system-independent to the extent that they refer to any human society trying to attain or sustain prosperity on this planet. They are therefore basic to any economic system. The creation of an economic system therefore involves the question of who will control or own these capital assets and how they will be managed and used to bring about the desired prosperity.

Predictably, the human mind has invented systems that range from one extreme to another: from a maximum of sharing between people to control by a centralized authority, or to a free-for-all system allowing individuals to accumulate capital and power for themselves. At the extreme of maximal sharing we have the example of the indigenous people in North America, who not only shared resources within their tribe, but also took care not to overexploit those resources, thus ensuring the sustainability of their system. The system included conventions about trespassing on the territory of neighboring tribes, which could lead to serious friction. But within the tribal lands the system worked well.

Among technologically more advanced societies we have the extreme control of the communist regimes that insisted on natural and most or all built capital being the property of government, while the rest of the industrial world wanted it in "private" hands, which of course has included the hands of powerful corporations. Countries with the capital in "private" hands are not necessarily democratic. Reading Placide Gaboury's delightful book, *Petite Galerie de Grands Esprits (Small Gallery of Great Minds)*, I was struck by his mention of the four types of government recognized by Plato: oligarchy, democracy, military dictatorship, and tyranny [3], and that Plato condemned them all. In my lifetime, it has seemed that democracy was the best, as objectively it has handled environmental concerns less badly than the others, and has protected human rights up to a point. But it has revealed many flaws in other respects, particularly in the failure of elected representatives to represent the views of those who elected them. So we might do well to pay attention to Plato's condemnation. But what else is there that might govern a new, ecological economy? Here I am groping in the dark, but believe there may be hope in some form of participatory democracy [4]. That also will likely not be enough, since we need a political framework in which decisions must somehow be evidence-based.

Few governments, if any, have dealt satisfactorily with the question of capital, who should own it and on what terms. The basic political problem is that private ownership can lead to too much exploitation, while public ownership is rarely if ever transparent enough. Capital can be held by government to follow its own whims, without it being held truly on behalf of the people.

What then might work in an ecological economy? To answer this even partly, one does well to examine what has been happening in human civil society these past 30 or more years. Two big economic changes since WWII in Western society have been the advance in universal public health care (with the noted exception of the United

States) and the increasing expectation of employees that they will receive pensions upon retirement. Public health care is a major expense for governments, though it only partly justifies the current high taxation rates in the countries that have it. The pensions, by contrast, need returns on investments to pay the huge annual bill.

Investment is inevitably tied to capital, in the sense that all elements of capital in an economy must either be held by one or a defined group of individuals or held in common. I suggest that investment by pension funds is an unavoidable consequence of human expectations in the current age, and that the major pension funds will be a feature of any economy that we could realistically envision in the short term. But this will not exclude government from intervening for the sake of social justice. Also I think that private investment by individuals and other investment groups will continue. Most important for a new, ecological economy will be to encourage employee-investment so that the proportion of industry or business owned by the employees will increase. The increase of ownership of enterprises by employees is discussed nicely by Alperovitz for the United States, where many Employee Stock Ownership Plans (ESOPs) have been developed [5].

But what then must be the changes in investing? Obviously investing must have a role in steering the economy toward sustainability. The good news is that this is already starting to happen.

Matthew Kiernan has brought to light and emphasized the importance of environmental and social (ES) considerations in investment, pointing out that the trends toward sustainability are increasingly evident in corporate policy. In chapter 4 of his book [6], he presents evidence from a series of studies indicating better average performance of stocks when companies take sustainability seriously and manage their affairs accordingly. This shows up in investment returns when portfolios (consisting of many stocks) are assessed in terms of sustainability ratings, which Innovest (Kiernan's former company) did routinely. One can then look at how an actual portfolio is doing and assess how it would have performed had the stocks been weighted according to sustainability ratings. On average, such studies lead in about 85 percent of cases examined by Kiernan to potentially or actually enhanced performance of the portfolio having the sustainability weightings. The negative aspect of his findings was that, in that same period, most portfolio managers in the investment business refused to consider sustainability ratings in their assessments of stocks. Now, however, Kiernan sees increasing numbers of those same managers having come around to include sustainability ratings in the weightings within the portfolios they put together (private communication, February 2017). This is very good news.

## Further political questions

The history of Western civilization has an abominable record on theft of capital, as was exhibited following the decline of the Middle Ages and entry into the Renaissance and then the Age of Reason. People well-placed in society were empowered to take over what had been common land and claim ownership of it. An analogous wealth grab occurred, though much faster, at the demise of the Soviet Union, at which time all capital was the property of the State, except for a few dachas and some trivial items, amounting to a negligible portion of the whole. When the USSR broke up, the most valuable built assets, such as the oil industry, were systematically grabbed in what must be the greatest theft in history. The theft of private property by the Soviets in 1917 was also impressive, but at least that was done in the name of the public and ostensibly for their benefit. One of the many Soviet failures was that members of the public were not given shares as legal evidence of their ownership of what was held in common for them by government. The same can be said of any Western government that holds wealth on behalf of the public. This same lack has been characteristic of government takeovers of capital assets everywhere, including in so-called democratic countries.

Democratic government has further failed in its grasp of public versus private interests, in that, when it has accumulated a property or business concern in the name of the public, it always retains the right to sell it back to private interests. There has been nothing to stop government from acquiring assets at very great cost and selling them into private hands at a much lower total price. Maybe some shares should not be tradable, but instead held by each taxpayer for his or her lifetime. We also hear too often of the privatization of water supplies, going even as far as making it illegal for people to collect water from their own roofs [7]. Such absurd and unjust occurrences could in principle be prevented if publicly-owned properties, enterprises and facilities were literally owned non-transferably by the public, who would themselves be the shareholders. Water resources must surely become part of such commons. The above dilemmas, as well as the more obvious ones, such as tax loopholes for the rich, are some of the areas where the ecological economy will have to improve markedly upon what we have today.

Next we must look at the kinds of shares that are available on the stock market, many of which involve ownership of enterprises producing goods and materials that are widely valued and used, while others include businesses such as stores that also fulfill important social functions. Then there are the banks. All such enterprises must be owned by someone or some named group or held in common by the public. There is nothing wrong in principle with investment. Even Marxists believe in it, though they think (or used to think) that all enterprises should be publicly owned.

Most investment, private or public, is risky. The most soundly run business can collapse through unpredictable developments. Therefore investors must seek protection from such risk by diversifying their investments. On the positive side, there can be huge profit from wise investment. With private investment, a difficult question is how much of that profit should return to the government, having regard to the risk element and other factors, and this question is reasonably dealt with in many jurisdictions. With regard to the ethics of investment, I again refer readers to the works of Hazel Henderson [8].

There are established developments in the stock-trading world, in which the "products," such as derivatives, have nothing to do directly with production. This question is discussed by John Michael Greer who refers to this sector of investing as the "tertiary economy" [9]. He points out that, following the 2008 crash, many of the billions in new money put into the economy to stimulate economic activity went into this tertiary economy, which is essentially unconnected with the production of goods and services to satisfy human needs, so that the investment is pure gambling. This tertiary economy has reached a scale within the current investment system such that it needs prompt attention. The basic reason is that it drains money from circulation in the first and second economies, which include all economic activities directly affecting human wellbeing. At the same time it enriches some of those who invest in it and benefits nobody else, though it circulates a huge amount of money within itself.

In conclusion, investment in productive enterprises will likely proceed in an ecological economy as it does today, but with an increasing focus on sustainability of enterprises that investors are willing to invest in. The tertiary economy would appear to require special new regulations or taxation to keep the money circulating within it in some ratio to the amounts circulating in the primary and secondary economies (Greer's terminology). I can see no objection to public ownership of capital, provided that it is truly public and not merely held by government. For vital supplies, such as fresh water, it would seem obvious that public ownership must prevail.

**Notes**

1. A useful but by no means conclusive discussion of substitution and other related economic concepts can be found in Daly and Farley's *Ecological Economics* second edition chapter 5.

2. National Roundtable on the Environment and the Economy (NRTEE) *Environment and Sustainable Development indicators for Canada* Renouf Publishing Ltd 2003 ISBN 1-894737-06-7. The Introduction includes the following statement: The development of these indicators is founded on the new economics that recognizes that the world's

natural capital provides us with services that are crucial to society. The expression *new economics* is also used nowadays to refer to the manner in which traditional economics has developed since the 1970s, though this is clearly not what is meant in NRTEE's statement!

3. Placide Gaboury *Petite Galerie de Grands Esprits* Quebecor 2002.

4. Dmitri Roussopoulos and C George Benello eds *Participatory Democracy* Black Rose Books 2005. Hazel Henderson *Building a win-win World* Berrett-Koehler Publishers 1996 chapter 11.

5. Gar Alperovitz *America beyond Capitalism: reclaiming our wealth, our liberty and our democracy* Democracy Collaborative Press 2011 chapter 7.

6. Matthew J Kiernan *Investing in a Sustainable World* Amacom 2009.

7. The acquisition of water rights by corporations can take place and has done so in numerous countries, whether through urgent need of funds by the government concern or through corruption. Such decisions would be almost unthinkable under participatory democracy.

8. Hazel Henderson *The Politics of the Solar Age: Alternatives to Economics* Knowledge Systems Inc 1988. Chapter 13 "Thinking Globally, Acting Locally: Ethics for the Dawning Solar Age" encapsulates Hazel's very general thinking on the transformation that must come.

9. John Michael Greer *The Wealth of Nature: economics as if survival mattered* New Society Publishers 2011 pp. 59-61. He defines primary goods and services as those provided by Nature, while secondary goods and services involve human labor.

# Chapter Six
## Wealth Creation

We humans have exploited the planet's natural capital through the use of tools since the Stone Age. The agricultural and industrial revolutions progressively accelerated this process. Resource exploitation has reached the point where efforts to rebuild natural capital have become not only necessary, but urgent. The desecration of the natural world, in combination with the huge increase in human population, is fast reducing the probability of a happy next chapter to the human story. Any fine future the human race may hope to enjoy depends on rebuilding what has been destroyed or allowed to decay, **and on keeping the peace while this is going on**.

The most obvious ways of increasing natural wealth, from a human standpoint, are: to optimize organic farming and increase the extent of its use; to plant or replant forest, enrich the forest floor and halt undesirable practices in forestry; to preserve the wild fish stocks of the ocean; and to avoid and prevent pollution of land or waters. It happens that such activities benefit all species, and fall in line with the new paradigm.

## Organic farming

The objective of organic farming is to produce high-yield crops of nourishing products that are the most resistant to disease and pests. Experience has shown that the optimization of the amount of organic matter in soil works to this end. The grower seeks to optimize the amount of organic matter in the soil for his particular choice of crops. The optimization is achieved through rotation of crops and livestock and by maintaining soil minerals through the use of natural inputs, including limestone and other ground rock powders [1].

The proper build-up of organic matter in soil can take many years, partly since soil and climate can differ greatly from place to place. Each grower must decide on a strategy—which crops to choose—and on crop rotation, the two factors that determine the rather long period to optimal soil composition. The organic content of the soil can be measured directly, while crop yields and quality, though dependent on seasonal weather, are the ultimate indicators of success.

Let's look at how good soil helps a plant to receive nutrients from the soil, and enables the roots to transfer new organic matter into the soil. In the natural state, carbon is absorbed in photosynthesis, much of it going into plant growth, while the rest goes through the roots into the soil. The mechanism for transfer into the soil is through the function of mycorrhizal fungi, which connect themselves to the roots. These fungi also secrete glomalin, a sticky substance that aggregates the soil into small lumps. Soil consisting of such lumps leaves narrow channels between the lumps through which water can more easily penetrate into the soil. The healthy soil is thus slightly moist where it needs to be to optimize biochemical development, which is further promoted by earthworms and other soil workers. The mycorrhizal fungi also convey nutrients to the plant's roots, thus completing a simplified picture of the astonishing biochemical world of plant roots and soil [2].

In his book, The End of Plenty, Joel Bourne states that since 1990, organic food sales in the United States have grown by double digits nearly every year [3], and that by 2012 the US organic market was worth $28 billion—more than double Monsanto's. The growing preference for organic foods is surely due to the absence of the chemicals used in agribusiness and the better nourishment provided by the products. However, the overall organic market stood at only 4 percent of food market value in 2014 [3], so it would have to sustain its current 10 percent annual increase to reach a modest 17 percent in the USA by 2030. With an ecosphere in peril, as it is now, much more rapid progress is needed. This author proposes a general goal 70 percent organic farming by 2040, which would have a considerable effect on $CO_2$ sequestration (see section below: the Rodale Institute's claim).

The situation for organic farmers is similar in other rich countries, where agribusiness is somewhat more productive than organic farms. In poor countries, however, Bourne mentions similar outputs for traditional farming and agribusiness. He also mentions the project of Hine and Pretty at the University of Essex, which covered 37 million hectares in 57 developing countries, and found that changing traditional farming to organic increased yields by 80 percent. One might therefore hope that organic farming in such countries could increase at a faster rate than has been observed in the USA.

In rich countries, farmers can afford the chemicals from the larger profits that agribusiness often realizes from its somewhat larger crop yields than those of most organic growers. Agribusiness can pour huge amounts of fertilizer into its fields, which the plants readily take up. The addition of chemical fertilizer nourishes the plants all right, but the complex, natural system ceases to function. The aggregation of soil ceases, the earthworms disappear and the plants no longer put carbon into the soil.

The full import of an ecological economy is to be seen in the picture immediately above. Organic is ecological because it sustains life to its maximum—processes that brought the world from its early plant life to the present. It also encourages biodiversity. Agribusiness does the opposite because it delivers a *knockout blow*, as one might say in the ring, to natural soil processes. It is also unsustainable, since it uses non-renewable materials. Its considerable financial profits arise from the absence, in our traditional economy, of the obligation to cost processes that do not involve financial transactions, namely: loss of natural capital from previously healthy soil; and chemical run-off into river systems and onward into the ocean. By contrast, organic farming has none of the above defects, but such farmers must nevertheless pay for the regeneration of the soil and face lower rates of return while all too often taking out considerable interest-bearing bank loans. Agribusiness has to pay for its chemicals but does not have to pay for resulting soil degradation. Could there be a less even playing field?

An ecological economy would underwrite the restoration of soil wealth through policies such as subsidies and interest-free loans. Here and elsewhere in this book I recommend that this be done through publicly-owned banks, which can be created in countries lacking one.

Credit Unions could also play a role here. A private bank that is also a benefit corporation (see Chapter Thirteen), should one such ever come into existence, could also play a role in supporting the increase of natural wealth. The present banking system could coexist in parallel, making the essential change more realizable politically in the short term.

Interest-free support to convert farms to organic growing could lead to a substantial increase in the numbers of farms being converted to organic.

## The Rodale Institute's claim

The Rodale Institute was likely the first to publish a statement to the effect that organic farming worldwide would sequester enough $CO_2$ to compensate for the huge tonnages of greenhouse gases being put into the atmosphere by the human race. Rodale's September 2020 White Paper confirms this remarkable claim [4]. This is not a message that should allow us to relax and say, "problem solved," as a great increase in organic farming will be needed to arrive at such an equilibrium, and also we have passed the point where feedbacks due to global warming begin to add to the warming itself. Nevertheless, Rodale has made a case that cannot and must not be overlooked—see Chapter 22, recommendations 6e, 6f and 7.

## Biochar

Biochar is a form of carbon made by heating organic matter at a temperature just above 325 C in the absence of oxygen. It was known to the indigenous people of South America for centuries before the arrival of Europeans. Some of the acreages that became very fertile in ancient times through the presence of biochar in the soil are still to be found today, such soil being known as *terra prieta*. The photo straddling pages 16-17 of Jeff Cox's book *Gardening with Biochar* shows an astonishing cut-away of the rich, black soil, *terra prieta*, at least two feet deep.

The structure of the carbon in its biochar form is that of the living matter from which it was made, which preserves the tiny channels and cavities of nature's design, permitting storage of soil nutrients and moisture. Biochar is thus an additive to soil, not a substitute for other organic matter. It works best in limited quantities, chosen to maximize fertility. Biochar also provides resistance to drought through its ability to retain moisture, which is a reason for adding it to soil that is already fertile.

Biochar is fast becoming understood and applied to growing plants, especially by gardeners, while its extensive application to farming and forestry awaits its production at an economy of scale not yet reached.

Biochar is also claimed to be great in its effect of increasing sequestration of $CO_2$ from the atmosphere. In fact the increased sequestration is due to the state of fertility, which has many components. The matter of additional sequestration through the use of biochar is discussed briefly in Appendix 4.

**Delayed benefits**

Delays in benefits are a feature of all natural wealth-increasing projects. It takes time to develop an organic farm, or to grow a tree to maturity. In the matter of sequestration, however, a young forest can pay an early dividend.

**Afforestation**

Afforestation, or tree planting where there is no forest, is a major strategy for increasing natural wealth that will sequester $CO_2$ during the growth period, two vital factors in the essential global future.

Afghanistan, for example, was recognized by an official in Ontario's forest service as a territory having widespread areas of good soil and water conditions for afforestation [5]. There is no shortage of labor in Afghanistan, though the long-term commitment of any land that presently has other uses could prove an impediment.

Afforestation elsewhere, especially in desert areas is of particularly great interest. The big questions are soil quality and water availability. In some areas, such as the Dalmatian coast, which was stripped of its trees centuries ago, the rainfall might just be sufficient for afforestation, but the soil eroded long ago into the Adriatic and would have to be replaced. The labor and energy costs of such a project would be high, unless some new system was invented to rebuild the soil and supply sufficient water to the young forest until it became re-established. A new Dalmation forest would surely bring about an improvement in the Mediterranean rainfall, at least in the general region of reforested areas. Climate models have projected drought through most of the land near the Mediterranean Sea so afforestation could be most valuable there, justifying large commitments of resources and labor.

An example of a small semi-desert that has been converted into a tropical forest in these last 55 years is Auroville, in south-east India, near Pondicherry. Auroville was founded as a "City of the Future," where people of all nations or religions should be able to live in harmony. Its planning and existence were largely the inspiration and work of a French immigrant, Mirra Alfassa (later known as the Mother), who had been for over a decade the main spiritual influence at the ashram in Pondicherry. The new town was formally given its mandate at a big celebration in 1968. The land acquired for the project was semi-desert, consisting mainly of red sand and sandstone. One of the earliest activities of the first settlers (1966) was to find water. Having found water underground, they were thus able to live there, grow food, and plant trees. The forest developed slowly, accelerating in the 1970s, as new settlers arrived, totaling 300 by 1973 [6]. The area is now regarded as tropical forest by many, with its monsoon in season.

Analogous forest creation is possible in many places, though soil quality and water will always be primary issues.

**The Great Green Wall of Trees to Halt the Advance of the Sahara**

This important project has come into focus again thanks to the publication of a biography of Richard St Barbe Baker [7]. Project results show that the replanting of Forest in the Sahara, given adequate feeds, can be successful, that some success has been achieved in Senegal, and that, by 2016, 15 percent of the 700-mile belt across Africa had been reforested. International cooperation could play a most important role in completing the Great Green Wall, thus building natural wealth for local communities, while addressing climate change.

**Afforestation in the north**

The northern tree line was, in the mid-twentieth century, the long, irregular east-west curve running across northern Canada and much of Russia, north of which trees of any size were rare. Global warming has greatly changed that picture. Around 2007 it was estimated that the tree line would shift 100-150 km further north, yielding the possibility of additional growth over more than a million square km in northern Canada and Russia. Such growth has already begun. Today, with Arctic ice disappearing, trees can grow naturally all the way north into the tundra. The question then becomes, where would it make sense to *plant* trees in those northern regions? The answers are roughly as follows: in the regions between the old tree line and the tundra, tree planting can be an ecological advantage, although forest fire control is a major concern because of accessibility. The further north one goes, one needs to consider the slower rates of sequestration of $CO_2$—because of the shorter growing season—and the loss of reflective power of the treeless areas once they become tree-covered—this is because snow in treeless areas reflects a considerable amount of solar energy back into outer space. A compromise within the tundra is to accept the enhanced sequestration where it occurs naturally and to benefit from the reflection of solar rays in patches where there are no trees. The northernmost land thus becomes a patchwork of forest and tundra. The case for planned expansion of forests northward from the old tree line is thus limited to the most accessible areas, where fire control is practicable [8].

**Super-productive forest**

The possibility, in a temperate climate, of making a forest area super-productive has been demonstrated in St-Lazare, Quebec, by the work of Dag Radicevic, owner of an 18-hectare forest lot. This area was enriched with donated natural waste from the neighborhood, enough to increase the topsoil from a few inches up to twelve feet over 35-years. The astonishing increase in productivity, for example, the annual weight of nuts per tree, and the considerable increase in the number and variety of flora and fauna, as well as the improvement in the quality of the trees, are evidence of the success of Radicevic's strategy. The super-productive forest (polyculture) deserves to be studied on a time scale of centuries, also in other types of climate.

**The Ocean**

The ocean is a victim of global warming, pollution and species elimination. Three things can be done to restore the ocean's riches: reducing ghg emissions, thereby preventing further loss of the ocean's alkalinity; protecting species by agreeing locally and internationally on limits to the fishing of wild fish; and planning and working to end pollution of the ocean.

**Cleaning river systems**

This is something the human race knows how to do, but too rarely does it to the needed degree. Run-off from agriculture and pollution from cities are the main sources of river pollution. Run-off from farms can be reduced by planting trees or bushes along the river banks and by changes in farming techniques, while industrial pollution requires demands by the relevant authority for control of effluents. Such means can lead to clear waterways in which pesticides and fertilizers are hugely cut down if not eliminated. There is a loss of agricultural area by virtue of shoreline and fence-row planting, but changes in farming practices can bring economies in terms of the amount of fertilizer they use.

An ambitious project, not yet achieved after many years of effort, is the cleaning of the Mississippi-Missouri river system, which spans a huge area reaching as far north as mid-western Canada. The Mississippi discharges its water into the Gulf of Mexico, where it has created a dead zone, one of the largest in all the world's ocean. These dead zones are areas so deprived of oxygen that fish and mammals formerly commonplace can no longer live there. The Gulf dead zone's surface area varies according to the season and has varied greatly and erratically over the last 30 years, from below 2000 sq miles (about 5000 sq km) to over 8700 sq miles (22,000 sq km) [9].

A major benefit from cleaning up the Mississippi will be to restore that huge area to living ocean, eventually supplying fisheries. The process of reviving an ocean dead zone may be slow, but it would seem a crime not to attempt it. Also, the cure would bring benefits for the agricultural and forest areas affected, as the quality of the land is critically important in our highly populated world. The work force needed to achieve these objectives might be large, sometimes a benefit in an economy guaranteeing full employment (see Chapter Seven).

The Mississippi basin project's failure so far, in spite of considerable efforts to deal with the problem, illustrates very nicely the difference between a traditional approach and a fully ecological approach. Perhaps the project has been aiming too low—merely to reduce the dead zone rather than eliminate it. In the traditional economy there is a tendency to limit such a project through financing: a generous-looking sum is granted, which turns out not to solve the problem. An ecological approach would require a thorough study to assess what needs to be done to succeed—and no doubt much such work was done—after which the plans would be made to assemble the needed resources and team management and move forward. It could be, in the Mississippi basin case, that much of the farming in some areas would additionally have to be converted to organic in order to succeed fully, while there could also be changes needed in methods of handling industrial effluent [10]. The object here is, however, merely to point toward elements of an ecological strategy.

Looking at the above planning processes, the big question is, "Is it worth doing?" And the answer is almost certainly "yes," because we are living in a crowded world, and it's going to get harder to keep things productive and unpolluted as the population keeps growing, so it's surely worth learning how to achieve this. And the Mississippi basin project could be a great test case.

New skills for a project such as this amount to challenges rather than barriers.

## Compost from sewage

This topic belongs to a class of regenerative projects that would do much to restore the imbalance of carbon between town and country in many areas of the world. Any large city has thousands of tonnes of organic matter entering its borders daily in the form of farm or forest products. How much of this carbon is eventually returned to the land that it came from? Some cities produce compost from food waste, but there is additional potential for recycling from sewage. The typical sewage plant ensures that its liquid waste, destined for the sea, rivers, or lakes, is free of harmful products, but the sludge, which contains the solid matter in sewage, requires further processing before it can be used as natural fertilizer. Currently, sludge is used to supply farms with fertilizer, but much is also sent to landfill. There are, in addition, several known and tested methods of treating sewage that provide solid fertilizer as an immediately usable product in addition to very nicely purified water. This field of study should be revisited, since the more advanced methods of sewage treatment could prove important in our ecological future.

## Land-use planning for a sustainable future

In North America, land-use planning has mostly seemed to be based upon short-term thinking, or rapid profit-making for development, with the result that in some regions much useful agricultural land has been built over, especially in the more fertile agricultural areas. Up until now, the consequences have not been severe, in the sense that there have been continental food surpluses in many if not all the years during which such building development has been surging ahead. Looking far enough forwards, the picture changes drastically. The large human populations are still increasing; several megacities are still expanding; and good farmland is still being lost to development in many areas, and to aridity in others because of changing patterns of rainfall, implying that farmland is bound to become more important in those areas where the rainfall remains plentiful.

There are, however, considerable areas not suitable for agriculture that would be suitable for building and manufacturing. The immediate need, therefore, is planning with a 30-year forward vision, which takes us into the decade 2040-2050, likely to be one of global food scarcity [3] (see also Appendix 2).

## Conclusion

This chapter began by pointing out the long-term over-exploitation of nature by humankind, and then ran through various entirely feasible ways of righting those wrongs—a new agenda to be followed. The acceleration of change to organic growing could take place at once; it is just a case of recognizing the need. It is important, too, to halt altogether the kinds of exploitation that brought us to the present crisis.

## Notes

1. Eliot Coleman *The New Organic Grower* 3rd edition Chelsea Green Publishing 2018 p.8.

2. Gabe Brown *Dirt to Soil* Chelsea Green Publishing 2018 p.24.

3. Joel K Bourne Jr *The End of Plenty: the race to feed a crowded world* W W Norton and Company 2015 Chapter 12.

4.  See rodaleinstitute.org White paper, September 2020.

5. Ontario Forest Service, personal communication, 2007.

6. Anu Majumdar gives a detailed account of the development of Auroville, in English, in *Auroville: A City for the Future* Harper Element 2017. This book maintains a strong focus on spirituality. It doesn't tell us, however, that most of the first 40-odd settlers in Auroville (1966-68) were from Europe and North America, and had come there because of dissatisfaction with the "rat-race" of careers in Western civilization and were looking for something more spiritual. For readers of French, see Jean-Louis Guébourg *Auroville, une cité en quête de Vérité* 2018. Guébourg tells us that the population had by then risen to over 2700 of which about 40 percent were from India itself, while France then Germany were the next-most represented.

7. Paul Hanly *Man of Trees* University of Regina Press 2018.

8. Prof. Yves Bergeron, private communication, 2017.

9. https://oceanservice.coaa.gov/facts/deadzone.html

10. The U.S. Government provided USDA with $320 million (USD) for this project in 2009. The 12 April 2014 issue of National Geographic published Brian Howard Clark's article, "Mississippi Basin Water Quality Declining Despite Conservation." The article also indicates contamination of the Mississippi's waters through effluent from cities.

# Chapter Seven
## Maintaining Full Employment

In a society maintaining full employment, it will not necessarily mean that everyone is working, but it should mean that anyone looking for a job should be able to get one within days, even if it isn't exactly what she/he was looking for.

That approximation in fact occurred in post-WWII Britain in some places where factories were fully occupied in the trade boom following the war (1945-55). In one city where the unemployment rate was 0.5 percent, the unemployed were described as those in the process of changing jobs. Nobody who wanted work needed to be unemployed for more than a few days.

An obvious reason for maintaining full employment is its social desirability; it removes the awful uncertainty that one can be deprived of being able to provide for oneself or others, possibly having to face great want. The traditional economic system provides less than full employment nearly all the time, and recurring periods of severe unemployment in its recessions. In poorer countries unemployment is often very high. In April 2017, a news article announced the lowest unemployment figure for the European Union in many years—slightly over nine percent. If that is a low unemployment rate for good times, then something is surely wrong with the economic system!

Comparative economic studies show that of all age groups the one from 18-30 suffers the worst in the Canadian economy, which is not surprising, since that age group has neither the political clout of the older adult groups, while younger groups have parental and legal economic protection. Opportunities for youth must rank high in the new economy since these young people are humanity's future. What chance is there for a healthy future if they are set aside? A good start will be full employment opportunities, and education without resulting debt burden and, if possible, entirely without associated debt.

Depression caused in part by unemployment was emphasized in an article in *Le Devoir* [1], with the title (translated) "Depression hits young Canadians hard." The article revealed that in 2012 no fewer than 150 thousand Canadians between ages 15 and 24 made suicide attempts.

An objection to full employment from an industrial standpoint can arise from the weaker selection of candidates available when a vacancy is to be filled, but I believe better education and training can compensate for this. I also believe that this will take care of itself in an economy that sustains extensive ecological projects, where many of those engaged in such projects are likely to be young adults, including highly qualified individuals who would in principle be available as industrial needs arise.

What of the transition from the old economy to the new? It will be essential to increase employment throughout the transition or go for full employment at the outset and maintain it, because any severe drop in employment could bring about social dissatisfaction, and even unrest sufficient to halt the transition.

Fundamental economic changes will lead to social stress and protest if there are job losses. And changing from an energy base of coal, oil, and natural gas will cause extensive job losses in those sectors, and lead to protests if there are not new jobs available. The coal and oil industries will not close, because these resources are needed for the manufacture of chemicals, plastics, and fibers, but the burning would cease, and this will greatly reduce employment in relevant sectors. Curiously, the profit over the lifetime of a coal mine or oil well will not necessarily suffer and might even rise, but it will be realized over an incomparably longer period, and the human race will benefit overall because these primary resources are needed in the long term and could otherwise be reduced to nil (or uselessness) within 100 years. The determination of industries to exhaust the world's oil and coal reserves is surely insane, but the insanity arose from the economic system itself.

If old jobs are disappearing, where will the new jobs be? And can we create jobs for everyone capable of working?

Modern industry can produce all the manufactured goods needed by the human race with fewer and fewer people as time passes, through automation and the use of robots. In principle, robots save humans from having to do dull, repetitive work and on that basis are considered a good thing. However, people need meaningful employment. The debate cannot be resolved here, but I want to mention two mechanisms that could be used to make arbitrary replacement of labor by robots less attractive to industry; both are new criteria for the taxation of corporations, the present criteria having never made sense to me. First, a system based on the profit per full-time employee would surely be fairer in principle, since it would create a scale independent of the size of an enterprise. It would also discourage the unnecessary use of robots. Secondly, there should be several tax thresholds, by analogy with personal tax, without implying that the levels of those thresholds or the tax rates would be similar. It would be advantageous to use the same system and thresholds etc. everywhere, and thus avoid the "race to the bottom" that is induced by the current system (see Chapter Nineteen). The system proposed here would also reduce excess net profit and thereby slightly reduce inequalities. Furthermore, a corporation would pay less tax or none in situations where the profit is modest and the number of employees considerable.

## Job creation in the transition to zero emissions

To create new employment, we have to go beyond the thinking processes of traditional industry. We are facing emergencies: foremost the climate threat and, simultaneously, the need to make our civilization sustainable. Luckily, facing both leads us in the same direction.

The new jobs that have to be created fall mainly into two categories: those that will enrich the natural world, and those that will be essential for the transition away from fossil fuels.

The transition has been receiving much attention from scientifically minded people and from the many activists who are convinced of the threats facing the world. An enormous amount of work will be involved in the transition. One could describe it as having three overlapping stages (or phases), which cannot really be separated: The first phase will eliminate all fossil-fuel use from primary energy conversion, except where carbon capture and storage is used in tandem with fossil-fuel burning. This includes all electrical power production. The third phase provides non-emitting machinery and other equipment for industries so they can continue their work without emitting greenhouse gases. The second phase is intermediate in that it provides, through non-emitting manufacture, the machines and other equipment required for phase three.

All three phases need to be subsidized at zero interest, as there will be costs and possible financial losses arising from installing new equipment or machinery in many industries.

The transition for offices and the buildings sector belong in phase three. One should not assume that only electric power will be used after the transition. Geothermal energy could heat many buildings, so drilling into the Earth's crust must also be emissions-free. The task of making that possible belongs in the second phase!

Plans for the three phases that re not already complete or well under way must be pressed forward. Any postponement could result in a situation of "too little, too late" or growing unemployment, which could have disastrous effects on the transition.

Many jobs will be created in programs to restore or augment natural wealth (see Chapter Six) and to restore the commons. These activities will continue long after the transition, perhaps indefinitely. This kind of restoration needs to be set in motion now. Certain projets could begin with little delay, for example, to accelerate the conversion of farms to organic status.

New jobs will also be created in infrastructure [2] and education.

During the transition, it will be possible to maintain full employment. Later, we could arrive at a new equilibrium at which all the ecologically necessary work is going ahead, but cannot provide full employment. Should that situation arise, then reduced working hours must be considered. This is nothing new [3].

The full-employment goal proposed here applies to developed countries with enough natural resources. Countries with few natural resources would benefit if richer countries invested in green technology there, within a framework leading to sustainability, not dependency. Setting up the ecological economy wherever it can be done is a good first step.

I believe a well-run ecological economy would adjust production to needs, which can surely be done democratically.

In general, an ecological economy would always look at needs:

The need to restore and/or improve the commons

The need for better infrastructure

The need to preserve biodiversity

The need for better, largely organic farming

The need to restore and/or improve forest

The need for improved education.

Feel free to add to this list.

**Notes**

1. *Le Devoir*, 18 January 2017, pp. A1 and A8.

2. Increasing built capital is most often desirable, though it can give rise to conflict within the wider world of all species when it destroys or

infringes upon habitat. Because the human race has so extremely expanded its numbers, the question of infringing on the habitat of other species is ever present in developed countries and those with high population densities.

3. An early book on the subject of greatly reduced working hours was W H Lever's *The Six Hour Day and Other Industrial Questions* London: George, Allen and Unwin 1918.

# Chapter Eight

## Putting an End to Fossil-Fuel Burning

It is not merely urgent, but extremely urgent that the human race stop burning fossil fuels. If we fail to do so, the Earth will pass through a tipping point after which global warming will continue without the help of our $CO_2$ emissions. This will, over time, lead to a planet without ice caps and an ocean level higher by a few tens of meters than it is today [1]. See also Appendix 1.

To reverse the huge ongoing bad habit of putting millions of tonnes of $CO_2$ into the atmosphere every year is a quite extraordinary challenge. Furthermore, the emissions increase most years, the average since 1960 being 2 percent per annum [2], resulting from increased industrial activities, transport, and global population. The situation is different for each country, but only a few governments have grasped the importance of taking action and have put programs for the necessary reductions into effect. The laggards are many and include the USA, which could replace its coal-burning power stations with renewable energy systems, thanks to the good state of technological advancement in that country [3]. Though many cities and states are replacing coal, the national policy remained until 2021 one of subsidizing the coal and oil industries.

Since many countries are routinely increasing their $CO_2$ emissions, one wonders who, if anyone, is in charge. The several occasions when there has been a decrease in global emissions over a few years prove that the human race can live without increases—grounds for optimism. However, emissions continue due in part to corporations wishing to profit from fossil fuels while the opportunity lasts, and to national governments who see themselves as competing commercially and/or militarily. Meanwhile, the route to a plausibly prosperous future is through international cooperation, de-militarization [4], eliminating ghg emissions, and population control [5]. All of the foregoing are necessary to attain a sustainable human existence on this overcrowded planet.

Fortunately there is some good news. Populations and local governments, even provincial and state governments are waking up and are starting to plan the needed reductions. The young, who see the world future as theirs, are rebelling in non-violent style [6] and a Swedish teenager, now (2023) mature adult, Greta Thunberg, has inspired a few national leaders and is supporting the "rebellion" wherever she can.

These developments have led to a few changes, such as a newly stated resolve to tax carbon emissions—now 25 years overdue—still awaiting international action. A carbon tax could gradually strangle the machinery that depends on fossil fuel, facilitating the transition to non-emitting technology. To achieve the desired result, one starts with a low per-tonne tax and increases it stepwise. NRTEE in Canada produced a fine first report on the tax that showed nonlinear effects when the tax reaches very high levels, above about $250/tonne. Increases in the tax at high levels produce less effect than increases at lower levels. The carbon tax today appears inadequate to achieve zero emissions soon enough. This could change if the price of non-emitting transport drops fast enough. An additional strategy designed to eliminate emissions through planning is introduced below.

## CanESS

In 2016, a new economic modeling tool, the Canadian Energy Systems Simulator (CanESS), emerged from Robert Hoffman's group in Ottawa [7], which had earlier produced the global economic model GSS, referred to in Appendix 2. The new model, CanESS, was designed to assist governments, provincial or federal, to choose policies that would enable the elimination of ghg emissions to be realized *in a minimum time*. Doubtless the CanESS could also be tailored to the needs of other countries.

Inevitably, such a tool can also be used to arrive at policies that would achieve the elimination of ghg emissions at the lowest financial cost. However, as Hoffman himself emphasized, cost must be a secondary consideration in a global crisis. Canadian economist, the late

John Hotson, once commented, "Could anything be more insane than for the human race to die out because we 'couldn't afford' to save ourselves?"

When the CanESS was in its early stages of use, Hoffman experimented with it (private communication, June 2016) and came up with and later confirmed the following very significant conclusions:

**The standard negotiating routes for the reductions of ghg emissions, namely carbon taxes or cap and trade, will not produce the final result of zero emissions soon enough to meet Nature's deadline;**

**Governmental policies are urgently needed 1) to convert all electrical production to non-emitting methods and 2) to eliminate emissions from all surface transportation.**

Hoffman selected the above policies, 1) and 2), because the needed technologies already exist. For example, the New York Times published on 20 September 2020: "The Age of Electric Cars is Dawning Ahead of Schedule." It is simply a matter of asking or demanding that the relevant industries collaborate in implementing a solution. The manufacturers of trucks, vans and cars would have to prepare to sell only non-emitting vehicles by a given deadline. Hoffman, recently deceased, believed that emissions-free electrical power generation and transport could be achieved in Ontario by the year 2040 and I support his view. His strategy would be to notify manufacturers of all types of vehicle that no new ones dependent on fossil fuels could be marketed ten years after the notification. This gives manufacturers enough time to redesign their products. Vehicles using fossil fuels already on the roads at the ten-year mark would then be phased out in the following ten years. On 18 November 2020, the decision of the British Prime Minister to forbid sales of new fossil-fuelled vehicles in the UK from 2030 was announced [8], nicely coinciding with the policy put forward above. Elsewhere, the same policy could be followed with the same deadline, though success will depend on adequate supply of suitable batteries for electric transport

61

and of hydrogen for other non-emitting transport. Fortunately, there is considerable interest industrially in both these areas at present. Additional factors in vehicle design that could contribute to success in the change to non-emitting land transport would be an emphasis on lighter vehicles and a strong discouragement of high power-to-weight ratios, which are now commonplace.

Alas, there remains a major source of long-term emissions from land transport, namely, within poor countries that routinely purchase second-hand vehicles from wealthier countries, and will want to continue using them for decades, unless some new strategy of persuasion and assistance interferes. This problem seems to have been overlooked, and must also be faced on the road to eliminating emissions. Steps in the right direction might be: stopping export of any but the most fuel-efficient used vehicles; and a demand by the world of its vehicle industry not to design and produce any new gasoline-propelled vehicles except the lightest and lowest in fuel consumption.

Firm decisions are now essential to accomplish what can be achieved by the earliest practicable dates.

**Cost**

Cost, in the parlance of an ecological economist, amounts to the resources and person-hours that are required to accomplish a task. The money merely distributes those needed resources. This very different attitude to money would predominate in an ecological economy. Should we even be worried about money? Few people have objected to the more than one trillion dollars spent annually on military production and to maintain the armed forces, expenditures that can end up causing death and destruction, creating refugees, or generating waste. The ecological economy will use resources to counter climate change and to increase natural, built, and human capital, and other wealth, the opposite of what military production and activities do.

Major projects that generate large sums of money could require us to implement anti-inflation policies. Full employment, as discussed in Chapter 7, does not have to be accompanied by inflation.

## The later stages of reduction of ghg emissions

There is no reason to delay efforts in other sectors of the economy where elimination of emissions may be more difficult. The sooner the necessary research and development takes place the better, as the emissions in these sectors must also be brought to a low minimum. A sector where work could begin at once, and where emissions are particularly high is production of cement for making concrete. The emissions are due to: a) burning fossil fuel to heat the calcium carbonate, which is the raw material for cement, and b) the $CO_2$ emitted by the carbonate during the heating. The heating could in principle be electrical (radiative), or from burning hydrogen, whereas the emissions from the heated carbonate are inevitable and consist of $CO_2$. In this case, the $CO_2$ is largely free of the other products of combustion in air, which makes it easier to trap for storage or later use. An example of its use is for the production of algae, on which much research has been done these last decades [9].

There has also been research on chemically new forms of concrete that can be manufactured without emissions.

Recently an emissions-free concrete block has been developed in Quebec and is being manufactured on a modest though expanding scale. It is based on calcium carbonate and eliminates the emissions by using waste (scoria, largely carbon) from the manufacture of steel instead of cement. The mixed, damp powders are compressed into concrete blocks that are then dried in an atmosphere of $CO_2$, much of which is absorbed into the concrete. The resulting hard-construction concrete is the first to be overall carbon-negative! [10]

By attending to every sector of the economy in ways such as have been touched upon here, one can envision numerous emissions-free countries within 30 years.

## Emissions-free transport

Emissions-free road vehicles will likely be electric or hydrogen-powered. An all-electric system would be limited by battery availability, while hydrogen propulsion will become affordable as the price of wind power declines, reducing the cost of hydrogen production by electrolysis. A mix of electric and hydrogen transport is surely desirable as there will always be the possibility of significant outages of electric power in an all-electric system, even where decentralized power generation has been established.

By contrast, air and ocean transport are not near a point in time where we can describe non-emitting futures. These two forms of transportation will be needed to continue international trade and tourism, and are discussed in Chapter Eleven.

## Countering objections to climate action

An argument that is heard often enough, claiming the futility of efforts, for example, to manufacture emissions-free vehicles, goes as follows: "If we need such and such machinery or equipment to run a fossil-free energy system, then we shall still need fossil fuels to manufacture the new machinery and equipment, because that is how the manufacture is actually done." The answer to this is obvious enough: a special effort is needed now to get manufacturing entirely off fossil-fuel use, since that sector will always be active in the foreseeable future. Maximizing primary energy conversion to non-fossil is thus a major priority, and eliminating fossil fuels from every type of manufacture must take place in parallel.

## Cities

Cities hold most of the world's human population and acquire most of the population increases. They also tend to be highly unsustainable and built on good agricultural land. Today, agricultural land needs to be preserved and improved because of the fast-rising global population; but cities continue to spread and sprawl over the best land, while areas of poor land that could sustain sizeable cities are ignored. Many areas of the world could find themselves short of good agricultural land before 2050, which could cause widespread hardship if no long-term planning takes place. See recommendation 4 in Chapter Twenty-Two.

In the meantime, there are cities undergoing redevelopment that can provide opportunities to make a whole section of a city sustainable, or nearly so. Such redevelopment involves every aspect of the locality: the overall plan, buildings, streets, parks, food growing ("urban agriculture"), schools, businesses, transport, energy, and consumption. Greenhouse gas emissions are being reduced in this way, long before the last ghg-emitting vehicles are taken off the roads.

In France, the city of Strasbourg already has several sectors fully functioning as *eco-quartiers* [11], that is, ecologically sound neighborhoods. The government of France has a national program to encourage such development [12]. There are also officially recognized eco-districts in at least eight other countries.


## Carbon Capture and Storage

The expression Carbon Capture is used in two senses: the removal of carbon dioxide that is already widely distributed in the atmosphere; and , the capture of carbon dioxide effluent from industrial plants. The latter is much less costly than the former, because the concentration of carbon in the effluent gases from industrial chimneys is very much higher than in the atmosphere.

Carbon sequestration from the atmosphere can best be achieved through organic farming and afforestation. Therefore, most or all the large-scale engineering methods of carbon capture from the atmosphere are controversial, since they have low efficiencies and/or significant environmental costs, so they would have a hard time gaining general acceptance.

For emissions of $CO_2$ effluent in industry, a whole field of applied science and engineering has also opened up under the general title of carbon capture and storage [13,14] A promising method of geological storage has been described by Howard Herzog [15]. The methods of storing carbon dioxide from industrial effluent have been relatively successful [16], though the energy required to do it, and the accompanying storage of the captured gas, greatly reduce the overall efficiency of the related industrial production. Carbon capture in coal-burning electrical generation is seen as an alternative to a huge array of solar cells or windmills that need electrical energy storage capacity to provide some power overnight or when the wind isn't blowing. Many experts now think, however, that the batteries of modern electric transport will collectively amount to a potential storage system of shared energy, such as would make it possible to avoid large electric storage installations.

## The importance of going forward

The optimum attitude for any nation is to reduce all its emissions as soon as it can to the lowest level possible. The sooner and more rapidly emissions are reduced, the greater the hope of a successful outcome globally; and as avant-garde nations succeed in reducing their emissions, more useful know-how will be available for nations that lag in this. The human and technological skills of all nations are needed to lead the way in eliminating ghg emissions.

This is how to meet the challenge.

## Notes

1. Wikipedia, "Sea_Level_Rise." The melting of Greenland's ice cap would produce a 7.4 m rise in ocean level, while the melting of Antarctica's ice cap would supply another 58.3 m rise. It does not follow, however, that the southern ice cap would disappear completely, even following runaway global warming.

2. A graph of global $CO_2$ annual emissions from 1900 to 2019 can be found at https://www.iea.org/data-and-statistics/charts/global-energy-related-co2-emissions-1900-2020

3. This author does not favor nuclear energy as a general option.

4. See Chapter Eighteen.

5. See Chapter Sixteen.

6. See for example: Extinction Rebellion.

7. The Canadian Energy Systems Simulator is the creation of Robert Hoffman and Bert McInnis, both since deceased, and their collaborators at WhatIf? Technologies in Ottawa.

8. Journal de Montréal, p.17. The British policy had previously been similar, but with a later date, 2035, for banning the sales of emitting vehicles. A few days previously, the premier of Quebec had announced a similar policy, but also with the later choice of date 2035.

9. Edible algae and algae for making biofuels can be copiously produced by the action of sunlight on water rich in $CO_2$.

10. Le Devoir 25 January 2023 page B1, article by Alexis Riopel.

11. https://www.strasbourg.eu/demarche-eco-quartiers

12. https://www.cohesion-territoires.gouv.fr/ecoquartiers          Under this program, the French Ministry responsible for cohesion of territories approves the status of a new EcoCartier through a four-stage process. The USA and Canada have an analogous system of certification of such ecodistricts.

13. Global Carbon Capture and Storage Institute
https://www.globalccsinstitute.com/
also recommended: https://en.wikipedia.org/wiki/Biosequestration
www.kisstheground.com/Carbon

14. Howard J. Herzog *Carbon Capture* MIT Press 2018.

15. *loc. cit.* Chapter 4.

16. *loc. cit.* Chapter 5.

# Chapter Nine
## Reduce, Re-use and Recycle

This chapter emphasizes "Reduce" because it implies more than "Take only what minerals you really need out of the ground." It also says, "Since the human race has far exceeded any reasonable exploitation of planetary resources and has caused so much pollution, maybe we had better live more simply." This may not be every reader's notion about how to change the world, but it is nevertheless worthwhile to examine what living more simply means, by reading the literature on "voluntary simplicity"—see Bibliography at the end of this chapter. This literature is far from entirely new, so here we will examine other matters that are not as widely known.

### Minimizing extraction

What may at first sight appear as bad news for the mining industry, that an ecological economy must minimize extraction, will in fact extend the mining industry's history of prosperity and greatly extend the possibility of human prosperity. Mining has attracted much negative attention because of various forms of pollution resulting from mining processes during mining operations and long after they have ceased. The environmental consequences of tar-sands extraction in Alberta are perhaps the worst on record. A visit to Kirkland Lake (in northern Ontario) in the period 1960-80, where there had once been six active gold mines, may have shocked visitors, as there no lake—it had been filled in with mining tailings! The tailings were, furthermore, contaminated with cyanide, making them difficult materials to re-use. Another example of pollution at mine sites arises when uranium has been separated from its ore and radium is left among the tailings. Although the quantities of radium are small, the fact that radium is hugely more radioactive than uranium renders the tailings toxic. Also, the radium emits radon, a radioactive gas that pollutes the atmosphere.

Slowly the mining industry is making progress on most fronts, so the transition to an ecological economy will not likely be a dramatic explosion of environmental virtue, but a gradual continuance of the present trends, with help from the new paradigm (see Chapter One) and a growing understanding of the meaning of increasing natural wealth. Furthermore, there may not be any decrease in mining output in the early stages of an ecological economy, since the poorer countries will continue to advance toward sustainability.

A key question for the ecological economy is: are technologies available that would make mining satisfactory environmentally? The answer seems to be generally, "yes," and much progress is being made to implement what can now be implemented. The pressure comes from jurisdictions that do not want their environment spoiled, and from the greater profit that can come from forestalling pollution. Regulation is playing a major role. In a fully ecological economy, the mining companies could increasingly become benefit corporations (see Chapter Thirteen), having a focus such as would not require much, if any, additional regulation. There will still be mining companies that take advantage of weak regulation to extract minerals at the lowest overall financial cost, but the picture is one of an industry in evolution—good news.

## Successfully reclaimed mining sites

According to Cornerstone editors Krutka and Jingfeng, some closed mine sites are now forests, farms, open spaces or public parks [1]. In some countries a permit to mine is not granted unless there is a full closure plan prepared in advance. The financial costs per site can be high, though the average is estimated at only $1.5 million (USD).

## Toward Zero Waste Mining (TZWM)

More good news comes from the announcement of Canadian Government support for clean technology development in mining and other resource industries. Federal funds devoted to the mining sector and matched by that industry will thereby have the opportunity to transform some mining processes, advance energy efficiency and reduce $CO_2$ emissions [2]. TZWM, involving 40 companies, is a strategy of the Canadian Mining Innovation Council (CMIC).

## Keeping track of extracted materials: resource accounting

Julian Ortiz Cabrera writes: "... the mining industry still suffers [from] an 'extractivism fever,' that is, the focus is still in the extraction process rather than in the optimization of the use of the extracted resource... in Chile, little effort exists to track the extracted resources to know what is its final use... I can see a complete absence of planning regarding the extraction of resources at a country level, that is, the Mining Ministry does not control how much [is] produced, but only cheers for more production... I can see a similar behavior in... most South American and African countries, and even in Australia.

"Europe has focused on a different goal, which is to ensure the access to raw materials to sustain their development." [3]

Resource accounting is a significant requirement of an ecological economy.

## Reduce, re-use and recycle

This catch phrase tells us to use fewer materials, to re-use products that are in principle reusable, and to recover waste for new manufacture. The reduction of material consumption often goes counter to the desire for more stuff. There are, however, ways of reducing that come with new technology. Multimedia—online— books are just one example. By contrast, technical advances can instead result in more waste, as happened with the rapid evolution of personal computers, each new model rendering the earlier models obsolete.

Re-use is almost equally obvious as a step toward sustainability. Used glass bottles require much less energy to clean and return than the manufacture of new ones.

After reducing consumption to a minimum and reusing whatever practicability allows, we'll still have immense tonnages of useful materials going to landfill, and this is where recycling becomes important.

Many industries, including mining, have integrated recycling into their operations, which can be profitable and good for public relations. See, for example, Annie Leonard's *The Story of Stuff* (Free Press 2010), in which she provides more than a dozen discussions of recycling. The materials to be recycled largely come from garbage, often garbage collected from large buildings whose occupants have little interest in making sure that the materials that might be recycled are clean. But cleanliness is only one relevant factor. Recycling metals implies being able to melt them and make useful alloys out of them, not easy when the raw material for recycling comes from a mix. In recycling paper, it is important to add new pulp to the pulp being recycled, since the repeat process of recycling leaves the mix with shorter fibers and therefore weaker paper. Recycling plastics is one of the most difficult challenges. Plastic waste comes in a mix of so very many forms. What can one recycle it into? Author Will McCallum sees a solution (or part solution) in not using plastic in equipping bathrooms, kitchens, main rooms, children's rooms, public spaces and workplaces [4]. His big message to remember is not to produce so much plastic, and this in turn conserves primary raw material.

An example of how recycling can operate with great success comes from industries that send metallic turnings from their machine shops for recycling. For example, an industry may use considerable amounts of aluminum alloy, and can send for recycling loads of machine turnings that are of a single alloy. These can be melted down and converted into solid bar, ingot or sheet of quality similar to the original. Such material, however, is very different from what is collected from city garbage!

Of particular interest is *extended producer responsibility*, an industrial system originating in Germany whereby producers of goods become financially responsible for the waste arising from packaging that they use. Under this system, producers tend to avoid unnecessary packaging, or packaging that is heavy or involves dangerous materials. In North America, where extended producer responsibility has not yet been generally adopted, people are being "drowned" in packaging (Annie Leonard's choice of verb), which seems ever to be increasing. Around the year 2000, ballpoint pens were still sold individually and one could test them in shops prior to purchase. Then, about five years later, they were all encased in stiff plastic packages. It seemed at that time there was nothing much left to put inside plastic except green vegetables and this has since happened to a considerable extent, with a conspicuous increase in plastic waste. Wrapped goods can also be put inside a second covering of plastic, and Styrofoam became fashionable as an underlay for foods; so the "plastic war" continued and is continuing, in opposition to what is needed in an ecological economy. In the last few years, pollution by plastics has become a major international concern, especially in the ocean, where the plastics reach the digestive systems of many fish, aquatic mammals, and birds, and pollute beaches and whole regions of the ocean.

Because of excessive packaging, failure to re-use and to adopt extended producer responsibility, municipal waste is excessive in much of North America, and is surely serious elsewhere; and it falls to the municipalities to dispose of it or recycle it. It has been estimated that between 88 and 96 percent of a city's garbage can be either composted, or recycled in five categories: paper, cardboard, glass, metals and plastics. If the compostable materials are duly composted, the rest is sent to landfill in the absence of any recycling. The recycling of any of those five categories is called "diversion," that is, diversion from landfill. In the USA, the city of San Francisco already had achieved 70 percent diversion by 2007-8, 77 percent by 2010 and 80 percent by 2018, and proudly continues on the upward path. The city of Toronto in Canada made some progress from 44 percent diversion in 2009, but got stuck at 52 percent over the years 2012-15. Many cities have not even achieved anywhere near Toronto's 52 percent. Obviously there is far to go.

The foregoing discussion of diversion illustrates the importance of an ecological economy, since the poor recycling performance of so very many towns and cities is primarily due to the financial cost of recycling, which is compared in the current economy with the cost of new materials, namely the cost of their extraction and processing of primary resources. Those resources are not valued for themselves, but only as the value added of extraction etc.

> Taxing primary resources appropriately rather than taxing value added and services removes the block, and this shift in taxation is an important step to be taken in the way forward.

A tax on lumber cut for wood pulp could be adjusted to bring the cost of new paper up to that of recycled paper, and both types would have the current sales tax removed.

## Summary

Humanity, especially in richer countries, needs to consume less—wherever the ecological footprint exceeds the biocapacity [5]. Re-use and recycling are essential for a truly ecological economy, and there is an increasing awareness that these processes are important. The financial rules and the system of taxation within the traditional economy stand in the way of attaining these goals. For mining, there is a prospect of government support for TZWM, and one should note that, in an ecological economy, primary non-renewable resources would be taxed. A proper overall valuation of primary resources will greatly accelerate the adoption of maximum re-use and recycling, as well as beneficial programs such as TZWM. Where recycling is inherently difficult, as in the case of many plastic products, restrictions on production may be needed, though a high level of tax on the primary resource could play a significant role.

**Bibliography**

Duane Elgin *Voluntary Simplicity Second Revised Edition: Toward a Way of Life that is Outwardly Simple, Inwardly Rich* William Morrow paperbacks 2010

Daniel Doherty and Amitai Etzioni eds. *Voluntary Simplicity: Responding to Consumer Culture* Roman and Littlefield 2003

Linda Breen Pierce *Choosing Simplicity: Real People Finding Peace and Fulfillment in a Complex World* Gallagher Press 2000

**Notes**

1. Holly Krutka and Li Jingfeng "Case Studies of Successfully Reclaimed Mining Sites." *Cornerstone* is the official journal of the coal industry.
http://cornerstonemag.net/case-studies-of-successfully-reclaimed ...

2. TZMW research and development will include: replacing diesel power with electric or renewable power; recapturing otherwise lost energy; minimization of waste, treating waste water and tracking water quality in real time; improving ore reserve definition to minimize waste extraction; and reducing various costs.

3. Julian Ortiz Cabrera private communication March 2017. Professor Ortiz Cabrera is a professor at the Mining School, Queens University, Kingston Ontario.

4. Will McCallum, *En finir avec le plastique* marabout 2018, chapters 5-10; translated from *How to give Up Plastic* Penguin 2018.

5. Mathis Wackernagel and Bert Beyers *Ecological Footprint* New Society Publishers 2019, especially figs. 3.1, 3.3, 4.3 through 4.8, and 5.5.

# Chapter Ten

## Ecologically Sound Goals for Business and Industry

One of the nice things about a nonviolent change from a traditional economy to one that is fully ecological, is that some things can simply continue as they are (more or less). This chapter will, however, focus on current practices that will need to change.

To make a profit in business, one needs customers or clients, and much good can come from efforts to satisfy them and keep them in this state. There are nevertheless several factors enabling corporations to keep their customers and yet harm the environment and human health.

This is an area where changing the mindset is particularly important. In the long term what is better for the ecosphere is going to be better for the corporation too.

### Environmentally damaging processes

Modern democracies have the immense advantage of nongovernmental organizations (NGOs)—often well informed on particular environmental matters—that have challenged and continue to challenge certain industries to do better for the environment. While the effects of such NGOs have been beneficial, not all enterprises take up the challenges, and serious environmental damage continues. Examples are many and include poor handling of radioactive or chemical wastes, inappropriate clear-cutting in forests, and oil spills.

The legal instruments for preventing serious environmental damage would appear to be already in place, though not necessarily fully used. When huge environmental damage has been done these last decades, as in a major oil spill, it has tended to result merely in large fines imposed on the offending corporation. Wouldn't the withdrawal of the corporate charter of the offending company be more appropriate? Surely, in such extreme cases, the shareholders should be obliged to restructure the corporation and seek a new charter, or sell their assets. A new board and a new charter, preferably as a benefit corporation (see Chapter Thirteen), could set operations on a new and more responsible course.

## The food industry and human health

Many countries have tight food safety regulations protecting people from dangerous substances in food, though the same scrupulous attention has not been accorded to optimizing the benefits of food. Examples are wheat milling, bread making and the over-using sugar in processed foods. In 2004, FEASTA published its Review number 2 [1], which contained an article by Frank Rotering, "Putting Human Health Before Profit." Rotering argues that human health and wellbeing are parameters that can be measured objectively, and recommends these as indicators and goals for a "new economy." He may not have been thinking of a fully ecological economy, but his criterion was excellent from the standpoint of this chapter. Indeed, the United Nations puts out periodic assessments of how various nations are doing, and human health or wellbeing is always on the list.

In North America, junk food abounds to the point that, if everyone suddenly stopped buying it, there wouldn't be enough good, nutritious stuff to go round! We would have the choice of going hungry or eating at least some junk food until the food industry had revised its methods so as to provide for us all really well. As things stand, there is increasing obesity, which the medics agree is a "problem," and a range of other diet-related complaints, but no visible political response from ministers of health. Meanwhile, junk food continues to dominate certain food outlets. More serious and dangerous are the medical conditions arising from the use of chemical fertilizers, pesticides and weed killers by agribusiness, and these are touched upon in Chapter Seventeen.

What then about junk food? Aren't people doing rather well in spite of it, and living longer, often much longer than their parents? Yes, they are living longer and, globally, life expectancy is still rising. An experienced physician once said to me that his observation of the human body over many years was that it was designed to last 95 years, by which time the nervous system was coming to the end of its design-life. There's likely some truth in this, but then, what about the centenarians? [2]

In the meantime, life expectancy is far below the aforesaid physician's best estimate, so there's work to be done: to reduce junk food; reduce dramatically the incidence of obesity, diabetes, arthritis and many other chronic complaints; and change attitudes so as to encourage meaningful and creative activities long past a conventional retirement age.

A change to an ecological economic system would facilitate all of the above, because the need to maximize sales and GDP would no longer take precedence over the need to optimize wellbeing.

Other aspects of food and human health are discussed in Chapter Seventeen.

## Industrial production

This topic is extensive and complex. Annie Leonard provides relevant material in chapter 2 of her book, *The Story of Stuff*, revealing many unhappy truths about industrial production. The emphasis here, however, is on new challenges on the road to an ecological economy. Nevertheless, a section on planned obsolescence is included below.

## Planned obsolescence

There are principles of industrial design, whose neglect can give rise to planned obsolescence. A good design strategy is such that the parts of a product will come to the end of their useful life (that is, wear out or cease to function) at about the same time, but if one or more of the parts are bound to wear out sooner, then those must be available as spares and easily replaced. Industries have frequently violated that design principle in the interest of producing some product at low cost, which facilitates its sale in a competitive market.

Planned obsolescence has been an insidious feature of western civilization, and its economy of waste. It was rampant early in the history of mass production and reached a point of high visibility in the 1950s when certain models of motor car rusted out after only a few years of use. This excess caused a backlash which forced the industry into more laudable habits. The moral would appear to have become: don't indulge in planned obsolescence if your product is an expensive capital item!

It wasn't long before integral designs were available for sale, in which the goods could not be taken apart for repair. The logic was, "Well, it's a very cheap item," totally ignoring the increasing volumes of briefly used goods being sent to landfill.

Planned obsolescence has once again found new life in the international trade in cheap goods. With trans-ocean trade, faulty goods end up in land fill prematurely, and the receiving country suffers the environmental and fiscal costs.

Planned obsolescence can surely be reduced more easily under conditions of local production (see next chapter), and waste will be reduced deliberately in an ecological economy. Responsible industries test their products prior to putting them for sale on the international market. An example for clothing would be "wear tests." It is clear that western countries have been accepting goods from certain exporters that could never have undergone a wear test.

## Deliberate destruction of new or useful produce

The deliberate destruction of new goods is not often reported, and has rarely, if ever, been a significant overall loss to the world economy. A few examples were given in earlier editions of this book.

## Industries of the future

So much has been written about modern industry that it would be superfluous to repeat much of it. Some obvious faults need correction and other already-cited authors have had much to say. Two other comments must, however, be included: Frank Feather's conviction that, to avoid an overcrowded world through sustainable development, one must bring each population out of poverty, which has been largely achieved in China [3], and a mention of the HANDY report [4], which addresses the subject of collapse of civilizations, a relevant issue here. Let us distinguish for a moment between the collapse of a civilization that leaves numerous survivors alive, but living in a primitive state, while another collapse can mean the extinction of the population. We can use the collapse of the Roman Empire as an example of the former type, since the Roman territories remained populated by descendants of the various regions of the former empire. Collapse leading to extinction happened more often in isolated societies, such as those of certain islands or the collapse of the European settlements in Greenland.

Today, the failure of the human race to create a new, sustainable economy will lead to the former type of collapse, whereas the failure to address climate change will lead to global extinctions.

What can we say about industries of the future? The avoidance of collapse must be a prime goal. We have looked at the criticisms of industries of the "industrial age" and have hints of the improvements that have been achieved thanks to the influence of forward-looking leadership within various industries, and the light illuminating the path of change by people such as Hazel Henderson. We therefore know by now that future industries must not pollute, or at least they will deal with any pollution they cannot avoid producing. They must not waste raw materials and must recycle whatever can be recycled. They must satisfy public needs rather than overproduce in the hope of windfall profit, and that human health and that of the biosphere will be prime goals. Their treatment of employees must be just, perhaps brought about by democratic management.

What else needs our attention? My guesses are: first, learning to cope with a general goal of full employment; second, learning to cope with new demographic age distributions; and third, grasping what is meant by deep adaptation.

Full employment, which I have tried to establish as necessary in a just world (see Chapter Seven), can give rise to many problems when a given industry greatly reduces the number of its employees. It has been obvious for many years that parts of the fossil-fuel industries will close down on the path to a society whose requirements are based upon green energy. The shift cannot be attained without substantial unemployment unless new organizations are created (see Chapter Six; and Recommendation 7). Even with such provisions, might it not become necessary for various major industries to reduce hours of employment temporarily during periods of difficulty in the transition?

The most general demographic age distributions in a world of steady or slowly declining populations are bound to be those without the large base of young people that high birth rates lead to; and note, global life expectancy is still rising. Somehow, the numbers of people employed beyond age 65 are surely going to have to increase; otherwise there will be a general shortage of pension funds, a situation already evident in many countries, though often not due to the demographic age distribution.

The most difficult adjustment for people and for industries could be that of deep adaptation (see Chapter 11). The concept is that, to avoid collapse, people will have to adapt to the conditions that the path to halting global warming will require, and this must surely also apply to industries. The automobile industry has, for example, decided to produce fewer vehicles in the year 2023. Very wise. But what kind of vehicles will they produce? Will these emit far fewer ghgs than today's products? What they sell in 2023 and the following few years will stand out among the polluting vehicles still on the roads until 2050, a target year for zero emissions. Has this factor been addressed?

## Notes

1. FEASTA Review number 2 *Growth: The Celtic Cancer* 2004. FEASTA is the acronym for the Foundation for the Economics of Sustainability.

2. It is now known that people who live to 100 have a super-neurone that the rest of us lack: *"Science et Vie"* Dec 2022 p.26

3. Frank Feather (futurist and business strategist), personal communication, 2017.

4. Human and Nature Dynamics (HANDY) Safa Motesharrei 2014.

# Chapter Eleven

## Globalization and Transport

Globalization is already here, and we can see it all around us. Products of international corporations can be bought almost anywhere. Name your favorite motor vehicle. Is there anywhere you are likely to live where you could not find it or it couldn't be serviced? Consider food for a moment. What are the fruits that grow near where you live? Are these the only ones available in the food stores you visit? Unlikely! And what about vacations? Have you noticed the number of choices offered? Or the number of people wanting holidays abroad? Evidently people like to have such choices, and few would give them up willingly.

A useful basis for opening this discussion is Richard Douthwaite's article, "Why localization is essential for sustainability" [1]. Part of his thesis argues that the globalized economy is unsustainable. Enter climate change and the fact that we must stop putting greenhouse gases into the atmosphere. How might we continue air travel at its present scale, let alone its increases? And how are we going to enable more and more container ships to sail the ocean?

The greenhouse gas emissions from air and ocean transport are significant, even if, in 2019, they only accounted for eight percent of the total. Today, the fuels for air and sea transport are barely taxed. For shipping, the tax rates are different in different jurisdictions, but everywhere the rates are very low relative to what they would have to be to discourage burning that fuel. Such tax structures are grossly inadequate for addressing climate change. Yet, even at the insignificant levels of the tax from a climate standpoint, the slight differences in tax level between one jurisdiction and another are sufficient to influence fuel choices by operators of airlines or shipping because of the intensity of competition in the global market!

Evidently, international trade and tourism are increasing without regard to reducing greenhouse gas emissions, which presents a thorny problem for modern trade in the climate change context. If, however, one looks at the International Maritime Organization, it clearly has some clout on the matter of pollution. Its mandate includes reducing greenhouse gas emissions and it is currently planning to put a halt to sulfurous emissions from ocean-going vessels [2].

Let us look for a moment at Douthwaite's remedies for globalization, in the framework of a sustainable civilization. Reverting completely to local production, though perhaps possible in principle, is unthinkably difficult, especially considering that certain types of production, automobiles for example, need to exploit economies of scale. Douthwaite therefore favored a plausible alternative, namely to localize production where it makes any sense to do so, but to leave the major stuff requiring globalized economies of scale. This choice he accompanied with much advice, in particular the disadvantages of local economies taking loans from outside their currency area. Within the ecological economy outlined in this book there would be no need for such loans, at least in regions having sufficient natural resources.

Even the modest degree to which Douthwaite would have us restore local manufacture presents challenges. But these may prove economically and technologically stimulating and, ultimately, satisfying to those who rise to the challenges. The most visible result would likely be that we would find ourselves wearing locally made clothes and eating mainly local farm produce, as in the 1950s.

Like Douthwaite, I had not been able to see an alternative to leaving many portions of production and trade globalized, though I have often questioned in my own mind the huge extent of such trade and tourism, and we shall therefore look at the matter of trans-ocean transport in this chapter.

Above all, we must face up to the problem of ghg emissions. A long-term future of transportation, including sea and air, cannot be based on fossil fuels. The first and greatest single step toward sustainability is the reduction of ghg emissions everywhere to a practical minimum close to zero. This step alone could bring the global footprint down to a level only slightly higher than the world's biocapacity—see Appendix 3 for definitions of footprint and biocapcity. To attain sustainability, further reductions of footprint could be effected by trimming wastefulness [3].


## Transport

Readers will have noted in Chapter Eight that government regulation is now needed to eliminate ghg emissions from surface transportation, as the needed technical breakthroughs have already been made. Eliminating emissions from air and ocean transport requires much further attention, especially if trans-oceanic aircraft are to continue to grace the skies and large vessels such as container ships are to continue to ply their trade.

There are three basic technical choices for non-emitting propulsion by sea or in the air: electrical, chemical, and wind. Human-powered flight is a continuing challenge to enthusiasts in this field, but it will not likely enter into the transport of passengers and goods [4]! Wind was harnessed to propel seagoing vessels for millennia, and it is used today by airlines that take advantage of the high wind velocities in the stratosphere. Chemically, the emissions-free recipes are fuel cells, or burning hydrogen with oxygen, so as to avoid carbon emissions and oxides of nitrogen. Burning hydrogen in air produces oxides of nitrogen in abundance, and nitrous oxide is an important contributor to maintaining the holes in the ozone layer. The burning of hydrogen with oxygen, with only water as a byproduct, has the important advantage of being neutral with respect to the holes in the ozone layer.

While the chemical option is likely necessary for long-distance air transport, short-to-medium-range electrically powered aircraft already exist [5], and we can hope to see some in service by 2023.

For long-distance air transport, engines based upon hydrogen fuel, whether of a fuel-cell design or direct burning, would seem to be the only present choice, because of the limitations of current battery technology. The "Airbus ZEROe" is one of three European airline projects based upon hydrogen fuel-cell power. It will have a range of at least 3500 km carrying up to 200 passengers ("Science et Avenir" March 2021 #889 p.28).

For ocean travel, the range of options includes wind and solar as supplements to combustion-engine power. As a temporary measure, carbon capture could be added to current propulsion systems. There is also a remarkable new cargo ship designed by the Swedish company, Wallenius Marine, which uses only wind power for ocean crossings. Their 32 Ktonne "Oceanbird" is powered by five telescopically retractable "sails" reaching to a height of 80 m when fully expanded. It can transport a full load across the Atlantic in 12 days ("Science et Vie" Jan 2021 #1240 p.64).

Wikipedia has a long article reviewing propulsion using hydrogen as fuel in twelve types of vehicle (or ship) [6]. The conclusions are limited from the standpoint of application to ocean-going ships and large aircraft, as the article only mentions the hydrogen-oxygen power system for rockets. Could a rocket engine prove practical for inter-continental flight?

Though much research is being undertaken in this field, even more daring, avant-garde approaches could prove useful.

For hydrogen-burning engines, an inexpensive source of hydrogen is important. Production of hydrogen by electrolysis of water depends partly on the cost of electricity and there is a prospect of very cheap electrical energy from wind [7]. A cost advantage in hydrogen production would stimulate more basic research into fuel cells. As for hydrogen-burning engines, work is needed on hydrogen-oxygen turbines. If burning hydrogen in pure oxygen produces temperatures too high for a given type of design, then diluting the oxygen with argon might be worth trying.

Liquefied fuels could be stored on board ships or aircraft, though liquid hydrogen storage would require special conditions, to prevent leakage of hydrogen when an engine is not in use. Liquid Hydrogen boils at about 15 K (-257 C). Even in a well-designed storage vessel, there will be a slow rate of boil-off in the form of very cold vapor. This vapor can be recondensed in a closed-loop small-scale hydrogen liquefier, integral with the storage vessel, a parallel development program. The alternative of letting the hydrogen escape into the atmosphere is risky because of the flammability of hydrogen in air.

A striking factor of the Wikipedia article [6] is the application of fuel-cell and hydrogen-burning engines for vehicles of every kind. The vehicles, however, are all similar in size and shape to what we have on the roads, rails, and ocean today. If we changed entirely our pre-conceived idea of what a given type of vehicle must look like, and the mix of modes of transport for different purposes, might we not come up with a new picture of transportion in which fuel cells or hydrogen-burning engines could have much wider application than anyone has yet proposed? This leads directly to the last and most important point of this chapter.

## Deep adaptation

The idea of deep adaptation comes from Prof. Jem Bendell, whose long, scholarly paper on addressing the world's present challenges concludes with the notion that the human race can only succeed in overcoming its present challenges if it is prepared to adapt in a manner he calls "deep," though he leaves the interpretation of the expression to the reader [8]. The interpretation adopted here is that we must not take anything for granted, not the way we will eat, the way we will be housed, the way we will travel, or how we will have to work, in order to halt global warming and arrive at a sustainable world. In the context of this chapter, it means **not** presuming we shall: drive cars such as are now (in 2023) offered for sale; drive long-distance fully loaded trucks on highways at 110 km/hr; ship goods across oceans in today's container ships; or fly across oceans in anything like today's largest aircraft. One reason for this is the uncertainty in the total amount of energy that will be available annually toward the end of the transition to zero emissions. The global renewable energy annual output, while increasing, has far to go to provide even half the output that has been available until now from fossil fuels. Though more efficient use of energy could decrease demand, one cannot assume lifestyles in currently prosperous countries will resemble those of today (2023) at all closely. We'll need to adapt to the best conditions that zero-emissions can provide and, while we don't yet know what those will be, we can be sure there will be important changes in transportation. For example, the approach with public transportation has been to make larger vehicles or longer trains, rather than to offer more frequent service. Smaller vehicles and much more frequent service must surely come back into the picture.

We've made a good start for road travel, by inventing the bicycle about 200 years ago!

Small electric bicycles, scooters, and motorcycles are in wide use in many places already, Asian developments having focused on short-range commuter needs.

Where do we go next? Is the forthcoming range of ,electric cars the needed replacement for their fossil-fueled predecessors? Likely not in the long term, since the recent new designs tend to mimic the thirst for power in what we already have on the roads. Such designs lend themselves to long-range, or inter-city traffic. But for large cities, these are precisely what are increasingly seen as needing to be removed from city streets. To ban them today would be unfair to people living in suburbs designed to require such vehicles, so long-term transport planning is required. The removal of private vehicles from some roads has been be achieved by redesigning whole neighborhoods, notably in Strasbourg, France, but also elsewhere, to fulfill sustainability criteria (Chapter Eight, note 11). Even better results might be achieved in the design of entire, new cities.

Fully implementing renewable power presents as-yet-unsolved design challenges, but these developments, even if costly, are essential to our future and will cost much less in ecological terms than yesterday's status quo. It is about saving the planet, saving humanity, and arriving at a better place for all.

**Notes**

1. In *Growth: The Celtic Cancer* "FEASTA Review number 2" ed. Richard Douthwaite and Jon Jopling 2004 pp. 114-23.

2. Le Devoir 22 October 2019 B10 an article from Agence France-Presse by Marie Wolfrom.
See also http://www.imo.org/fr/pages/default.asp

3. www.footprintnetwork.org/resources                    Also Mathis Wackernagel and Bert Beyers *Ecological Footprint: Managing our Biocapacity* New Society Publishers 2019.

4. https://en.wikipedia.org/wiki/History_of_human-powered_aircraft

5. Israel's young company Eviation's "Alice" is an electrically-driven aircraft that can cruise at 447 km/hr and take a payload of 1100 kg a distance of 1050 km. *Israël-Hayom* 3 October 2020 newsletter.    See also:            https://www.rolandberger.com/en/Point-of-View/Electric-propulsion-is-finally-on-the-map
Wikipedia lists over 50 other battery-powered aircraft, not counting hybrids, at various stages of experimentation and trials in a dozen different countries. Harbour Air tested its first plane designed to carry passengers between Vancouver and Victoria, BC, 10 Dec 2019.

6. Wikipedia: "Hydrogen vehicle."

7. Inventor J M J Varga is designing a new horizontal axis wind turbine to reduce considerably the cost of producing electric power. Patents pending. Private communication, 2022. Mr Varga is the former president of Crosrol, Halifax, England.

8. Jem Bendell, "Deep Adaptation: a Map for Navigating Climate Tragedy," IFLAS Occasional paper 2, 27 July 2018.

# Chapter Twelve
## Advertising and Consumerism

Many people dislike advertising, yet it is both essential to commerce and legitimate. Businesses need to advertise what they have to offer, a factor older than the banking system. The problem is in the details. Some critics complain that ads spoil their view of things. They don't like placards in public places, especially where they obstruct the view of some splendid architecture, or of verdant countryside. Others don't like having films on TV, or broadcast concerts or plays interrupted by a "commercial." They believe that a time sequence should not be interrupted in that way. Others dislike the intrusion of commerce into their private space, and advertising can surely be an intrusion. Yet others dislike commercial activity on days that they consider sacred, or times of rest.

All these views have validity, but not everyone would be in agreement with abolishing intrusive advertising or commercial placards. And besides, some say of the media, "How would you pay for the programs you watch on television or listen to on radio if it weren't for advertising?" And that too is a valid question.

Advertising had already established important goals and methods prior to the invention of the internet. The arrival of the internet gave advertising a major new, ever-dynamic field of operation, with extensions and complications made possible by the new technology, and the speed of transmitting its messages. But the impact of all this goes beyond what this chapter can encompass.

What then needs to be addressed here and now?

Advertising has also played a major role in establishing overconsumption, in creating the society of waste, and to today's high global footprint. It has not been alone in this, but here let's simply look at what must change in advertising if a sustainable world is ever to be achieved.

The advertising industry has systematically developed methods of inducing people, through their ads, to want to own things or buy things that they do not need, or how to improve upon what they already have. The incessant message is that this product (whatever) is essential to you or that you cannot really live without it, or that your happiness depends on having it. Juliet Schor has written extensively on this subject and can testify to a relatively new addiction, the addiction to shopping. Her descriptions of waste are graphic.

But it gets worse. The psychological craft of advertising can also persuade you to purchase products that are not good for your health. Cigarettes are one obvious example, but there follows a panoply of food products, mainly processed foods, that are far from optimal. We call it the junk food industry, not intending to mean that any given item is poisonous, merely that it doesn't contribute to nourishment in the needed variety and proportions for human health. Much research and development goes into processed foods, which must then be advertised so as to bring in profit. And I daresay most of these products are completely harmless if taken rather occasionally, and taken by young people in great health. But, consumed often or consistently by people of any age, some of those products can prove very harmful in the long run.

Remedial action against the practices and trends indicated above would seem essential for a sustainable economy, most especially now as the human race must direct its attention cooperatively to prevent a climate transition. Health will be vitally important.

I present no answers in this area, and ask readers to come up with their own ideas, for public debate.

But I will risk an umbrella proposal: that changes in advertising be planned so as to place a strong emphasis on health. May 6, 2014, MacLean's Magazine published an entire issue on sugar, with the heading writ large on the cover: *Death by Sugar*. The issue spelled out in detail the various ways in which the food industry slowly kills some people through an excessive use of sugar, supplied in small or large amounts in most processed foods (including drinks). I subsequently read the labels on all salad dressings offered at a supermarket, and was surprised to find they all contained sugar. It is surely such widespread use of sugar that can make its effects deadly.

My second umbrella suggestion would be that advertising companies in future be registered as benefit corporations (see Chapter Thirteen), so that the objectives allowed and encouraged by their charters could harmonize with the new paradigm. This then raises the question of what to do about advertising companies that already have their license to practice their arts.

Of all the changes needed on the road to sustainability, those in the advertising industry are the least discussed as I write (in 2023), if indeed they are discussed at all.

## The consequences of declining consumerism

It is perhaps time to take a first look at the question of production and employment in a world of declining consumerism, one where people will buy what they really need and no more, since this is the needed trend. Voluntary simplicity as a way of life could make a huge impact on consumerism in a generation or less. The impact of such change will affect industries, employment in those industries and the retail trade, and it is not too early to give thought to how to maintain full employment in such circumstances.

## Bibliography

Terry O'Reilly and Mike Tennant *The Age of Persuasion : How marketing ate our culture* Alfred A Knof 2009.

Juliet B Schor *The Overspent American: Upscaling, Downshifting and the new Consumer* 1996.

Juliet B Schor *Born to Buy: The Commercialized Child and the New Consumer Culture* 2005.

# Chapter Thirteen
## Encouragement of Benefit Corporations

A benefit corporation is one whose corporate charter includes goals that are beneficial to humanity and/or the environment in addition to the goal of profit-making. In this way the benefit corporation differs very distinctly from traditional corporations, which legally have only the responsibility to make profit. Corporations can be and are subjected to regulations, which force them to maintain certain environmental or other standards, but the benefit corporation would in principle conform of itself with a regulation its charter already required.

To establish benefit corporations in any given jurisdiction requires new legislation. The idea took root first in Maryland, which became the first state, not only in the USA but in the world, to pass the required legislation [1]. This historic event, which passed unnoticed by most people, opened a new channel of hope in the development of future industry and businesses, since the benefit corporation will of itself conduct its business in accord with the environmental and/or social needs of the world community, as expressed in its charter.

The Maryland legislation came into effect in October 2010, to be followed by New Jersey and Hawaii, Vermont and Virginia in 2011. There are now 35 States that have passed such legislation as well as the District of Columbia [2].

In general, the purposes of a benefit corporation include that it

* shall create public benefit, and

* shall have the right to name specific public benefit purposes.

The registration of new benefit corporations in jurisdictions that have passed the necessary law is therefore a step toward the development of a sustainable economy worldwide.

The spread of analogous legislation to other jurisdictions has begun, though it has been slow, yet it remains much to be encouraged. On 22 December 2015, Italy's government approved a Benefit Corporation law, making Italy the first government outside the United States to take this step [3]. A benefit corporation in Italy will be known as *una Società Benefit*.

In 2018, Colombia became the first country in Latin America to pass legislation enabling the foundation of benefit corporations [2].

## B-corporations

The expression *B-corporation* is confusing because it can be an abbreviation for *benefit corporation*, but more properly means a corporation that has been certified as having maintained certain environmental standards [3]. The difference is significant, because B-corporations are certified corporations that have the usual legal basis requiring their directors only to make profit for their shareholders, and may only be conforming with given environmental standards for the sake of reputation. B-corporation certifications have been widespread and numerous, which could easily have a retarding effect on the introduction of benefit corporations worldwide.

## Notes

1. http://www.futurepolicy.org/business-priorities/maryland-benefit-corporations/

2. Benefit corporation Wikipedia

3. https://www.ecclblog.law.ed.ac.uk/2017/03/31/the-legacy-of-b-lab-italys-societa-benefit/

# Chapter Fourteen

## Banking Requirements

Chapter Four Introduced the general notion that in moving to an ecological economy it will be necessary to choose a banking system and a monetary system that will enable the economy to become sustainable. The system will have to finance wealth-creating projects that will not pay dividends in the short term, and will also not exploit organizations or individuals to their disadvantage.

**Funding important projects**

For many years I believed that the way to fund important projects, such as are outlined in Chapter Six, is through publicly owned banks. It seemed important to have a publicly owned bank in every single-currency area. I consulted Paul Hellyer [1] on the matter, and he replied that had been his opinion for years. Years later, Ellen Hodgson Brown's book, *The Public Bank Solution* (2013), reinforced this idea. Her book states that 45 percent of banks are publicly-owned in Brazil, 60 percent in Russia, 75 percent in India, and 69 percent in China—the BRIC countries [2]. The four countries had, at that time, 41 percent of the global population, a very significant fraction of publicly-owned banks, and go-ahead economies. It will be important to keep track of their progress towards adopting sound ecological principles. Chapter Twenty-One is a first look at this question, one that will require sound political leadership. Progress could be greatly hindered by destructive action, such as that of Brazil's President, Jair Bolsonaro, whose department of agriculture had his approval to conduct a militarily supported action to destroy the Amazon forest, where the damage was already (in 2020) colossal [3]. Brazil's election of President Luiz Inacio Lula da Silva in 2022, however, promises a turnaround for the Amazon (Angus Hervey and Amy Rose, in "23 good news stories…" Dec. 2022).

Funding important projects, as mentioned above, will also help to maintain full employment.

The Bank of Canada has been publicly owned since 1938 and was used to fund Canada's very considerable participation in WWII. Because loans were at very low interest, the debt burden was small and debts were paid off after the war without disastrous results, even though the level of prosperity was modest. By contrast, the Bank of Canada was not used to ease the privations of the depression from the time it was founded, March 1935 until after it became the government's own bank in 1938. In all, the depression lasted for ten years during which no Canadian federal government saw fit to take action as President Roosevelt had done in the United States, through his New Deal.

In the post-war world an arrangement was struck between capitalist countries and the Bank of International Settlements (BIS) in Basle, Switzerland, whereby national banks would no longer issue new money at nominal interest for government purposes [4].

Enter COVID-19, the confinement of people in their homes, closure of many businesses and loss of jobs on a scale unimagined, with thousands of individuals and families driven to zero income. Governments, faced with the immediate prospect of vast numbers of people unable to buy food or pay for their lodgings, found ways to provide large sums of money to keep the lifeboat afloat, incurring a large debt without major debt burden. The scale of the help provided by the government of Canada was large (see Chapter Four, section: Times of Stress). Similar action was being taken in other countries, many of which did not have publicly owned banks, so we must await a historic perspective to find out whether, overall, the existence of publicly-owned banks made an important difference.

A truth emerging from the economic pain caused by the virus would seem to be as follows: governments will react appropriately to an emergency by generating relief funds on a large scale if, by not doing so, the results would be sufficiently terrible.

The important question then becomes: **will governments recognize that low-interest financing is needed to address climate change**? Failing to do so would ultimately be hugely worse than the long-term

94

consequences of COVID-19, though the suffering would be spread over decades or centuries.

Somehow, we still have to convince many national governments that climate change is an emergency needing their full attention.

## A second look at the pandemic

While we may well praise governments for generous action during the pandemic, the unemployment caused by official responses to the virus could have been much less severe if governments had projects underway, or ready to start, such as are proposed in Chapter Six, and other projects such as will also be needed to address climate change.

## Banking reform or fiscal and monetary reforms?

Independently of the urgent need for an ecological economy, the case has been made for reform in banking practices. The evidence is that the system as currently operated slowly drives people and governments more and more into debt [5]. Traditionally, a loan may continue to collect interest as long as the capital is not repaid. For example, it became clear from international loans to poor countries in the post-WWII years that many countries were in effect repaying much more than they could afford because interest was paid over many years. A review of the terms for interest-bearing loans is needed. This subject has also been touched upon in Chapter Four, in the section on Debt burden. A contrary view is that the problem just outlined is really rooted in governments' fiscal policies and the central banks' monetary policies, which could undo the damage caused by the BIS deal. I would counter that there are forms of exploitation in bank policies that would not necessarily be addressed in revised fiscal and monetary policy, and addressing them would bring justice, a factor that is clearly part of the brighter future sought by activists.

## Parallel currency

A parallel currency is one that is additional to a country's official currency, and is approved by government, and controlled by government. To illustrate, currency of this kind could have been created by the Irish government to support its economy during a period of hard times within the European Union. The Union had been created without a system of wealth redistribution, and thus had no ready means to compensate the accumulation of currency in the Union's most prosperous regions. An Irish euro parallel to the official euro, but not transferable to anywhere outside Ireland, could in principle have relieved the difficulties experienced in Ireland at that time. In this example, the parallel currency would be legal tender within Ireland.

A parallel currency might also be useful for funding projects aimed at wealth creation. Since the funds would not be transferable into other national currencies, the additional money in circulation would likely not cause the official national currency to be devalued in foreign currency exchanges during the operation of the said projects.

## Private (or local) currencies, and cryptocurrencies

A private currency is one that is created and used (usually in a single-currency area) that is independent of the government's approved currency. Private currencies have a long history that predates government-regulated official currency and, today, many such are providing people with spending money in hard times.

Most private currencies today are local, and unofficial. Private currency is not legal tender, and in some countries private currencies are illegal. Nevertheless, there are many private currencies in use today, and they continue as long as they bring benefit to the localities where they are used.

Cryptocurrencies, by contrast, are not considered currencies by some economists but, rather, a digital form of token coins or scrip, because they do not conform with the four fundamental functions of money [6]. The value of cryptocurrency is highly volatile; nevertheless one of them, Bitcoin, though volatile, has already become important in trade, and one government has declared Bitcoin to be legal tender within its jurisdiction [7].

## An example of an unofficial, local currency

A system not requiring government involvement was invented by Michael Linton in 1983 for the community in Courtenay, British Columbia, which was stricken by unemployment at the time. This Local Exchange Trading System (LETS) involves membership and the new unit of currency was chosen to have the same value as the official Canadian dollar, though the new currency existed only as numbers in a computer. Trades between members involving LETS dollars were recorded by a volunteer through communication by telephone. Membership in the LETS system was free, and it was not necessary to open one's LETS account with a deposit; it could equally be opened with a debit. There was no reward for a credit balance nor interest payable on debits. A reason for the relative success of the system was its flexibility, since any trade could be carried out using both the official and LETS currencies. The traders agreed on the price, and on how much of that price would be paid in LETS. The system brought increased prosperity in Courtenay, and was soon copied in other places, often with variants on how it was operated. Today there are hundreds of LETS-type trading groups in many different countries, mainly in Europe, Africa, South America, and Australia, often with local names, other than "LETS." The Australian Government has supported LETS in several ways.

## Notes

1. The late Hon. Paul Hellyer was both in business and politics, holding ministerial positions in the Canadian government from 1963-69. He was a founder of the Committee on monetary reform that opposed the restraints imposed upon the Canadian government by its agreement with the Bank of International Settlements as described in this chapter. He was author of *Jobs for All: Capitalism on Trial*; *Funny Money: A*

*Commonsense Alternative to Mainline Economics*; *Surviving the Global Financial Crisis: The Economics of Hope for Generation X; A Miracle in Waiting: Economics that Make Sense*, and much else.

2. The nations formerly known as the BRIC countries added South Africa to their group some years ago and are now called BRICS.

3. Article circulated by Avaaz via the internet, 24 July 2019, and many press articles in the ensuing days.

4. The Agreement with the BIS essentially prevented Canada from using its National Bank from being used for a range of federal purposes, and led rapidly to huge federal indebtedness.

5. Louis Gill "Les dettes souveraines et la domination des marchés financiers" (Sovereign debts and the dominance of financial markets) in *Sortir de l'économie du désastre* eds Bernard Elie and Claude Vaillancourt *M*éditeur 2012 pp.77-89.

6. Numerous reliable, recent references can be found on the internet by searching for crypto currencies, private currencies, etc.

7. Since governments alone can declare a currency as 'legal tender,' it is unlikely that any private company using crypto currency would find that currency to be legal tender. El Salvador's decision to declare Bitcoin legal tender creates a rare exception. See internet: George Selgin author of "Paul Krugman and the Ersatz Theory of Private Currencies" 9 June 2022.

# Chapter Fifteen
## Defining and Restoring the Commons

The expression - may be less familiar to young people today than it was to their parents or grandparents. In England of the Middle Ages, the expression was widely understood, since there were common grazing lands, and land that was cultivated in common by serfs, people who were not paid but shared in the wealth of the harvest. During my own lifetime, there was still much common grazing on the British moorlands, for example in Yorkshire and in Scotland including the Island of Lewis, off Scotland's northwest coast, and it is likely unchanged. The commons were all over the open land, except where someone had legally obtained exclusive rights to some property or other.

Thus, the commons are intertwined with the law and, in this age of increasing interdependence, legal agreements must sometimes be made to define certain internationally shared commons and strike a deal on how such commons should be respected or maintained. The legal department of the United Nations Environment Program (UNEP) has this to say, by way of definition: "The 'Global Commons' refers to resource domains or areas that lie outside of the political reach of any one nation-state." It then identifies the four global commons: the High Seas; the Atmosphere; Antarctica; and Outer Space. The ocean bed could well be considered for addition to this list [1]. See also Susan J Buck, in Bibliography at the end of this chapter.

The discussion here, however, must go much further than that, to include commons in every land, even if no other state currently has the prospects of rights there. But surely such transnational rights already exist in plenty, because of investment arrangements or treaties, since a corporation may purchase land in another country, if so permitted either by such a treaty or special arrangement. It then matters very much what the buyer does with that land, which can range from land restoration or improvement to pollution or other ruination. The same applies to a buyer already a national of that territory.

For the purposes of this chapter, therefore, I shall adopt the widest possible interpretation of *commons*, to include not only the global commons as defined by UNEP. Only a few centuries ago, any land or water under the customs of aboriginal peoples would have been shared in common, not across a continent, but throughout a tribal area. A continent was therefore at one time a patchwork of commons. In this way, we shall include waterways, lakes and every type of territory. My proposal therefore harks back to the unwritten but well-understood conventions of aboriginal peoples in the Americas, and these have the huge advantage of respect for the land and waterways, exactly what is needed by humanity at large, now that its numbers have overflowed the basket. A new relationship with aboriginal peoples will help realize such goals [2]. The rest will lie in the details. It takes little space to enumerate the possibilities.

Farmland and forest can be rendered more fertile. The processes are such that increase the carbon content of soil. This applies also to formerly good land that was allowed through dubious practices to deteriorate, or to land that never was fertile.

Waterways can be cleaned up, with measures to prevent unwanted chemicals from entering the water. If waterways are clean, the lakes or ocean they flow into will eventually be clean.

Air can be rid of excess carbon dioxide by eliminating emissions from fossil fuels and by sequestration of atmospheric carbon dioxide. Ceasing to burn burning fossil fuels will also have the beneficial effect of eliminating most oxides of nitrogen.

Species can be preserved through judicious attention to habitat. Various new measures can be adopted to eliminate the unnecessary deaths of birds.

The sea bed can be protected from trawling and the ocean can be protected from other indiscriminate overfishing.

Intense irradiation of the ionosphere with electromagnetic radiation for the purposes of military developments can be halted forthwith.

Much more attention can be given to the elimination of contamination of outer space in the neighborhood of our planet, with special efforts not to contaminate it further.

In an ecological economy, all of these can be attended to, and it is vital that they not be neglected. The profit in all these cases is long-term.

## Managing a commons

So far we have looked at what might need improving in the commons, but no word on management. No chapter even mentioning the commons should omit mention of Elinor Ostrom, who shared the 2009 Swedish National Bank's Prize in Memory of Alfred Nobel. Her first book, on governing the commons, 1990, received its 29th printing in 2011, while her last book, 2007, co-edited with Charlotte Hess, gives us "eight principles for managing a commons" on page 8. See Bibliography.

When it comes to detailed studies on such management, one finds that the work is generally local, and different in detail from place to place. One would thus require a major volume to explain all the workings globally. For this reason, I go no further here than to supply some bibliography.

## Afterword

Because of climate change and the huge global population, it follows that growth of trees and plant life is more essential than ever, and it follows from this that any new farm or forest land or green space that is built upon, no matter whether for roads, buildings or parking lots has a negative effect on the commons, and therefore on the ecological balance of the entire world.

## Notes

1. Guy Standing, "How private corporations stole the sea from the commons," Zuma Press Inc. 28 July 2022. See also: Bibliography

2. The work of the Commission on Truth and Reconciliation in Canada and its Calls to Action (2015) form a start to this very necessary process. As a result, the Government of Canada at this time is working to replace the Indian Act of 1876, which is widely thought to be a product of colonialism and, as such hugely undesirable.


## Bibliography

Susan J Buck, *The Global Commons: An Introduction*, Routledge 2017

Ostrom, Elinor (1990) *Governing the Commons: The Evolution of Institutions for Collective Action* Cambridge University Press ISBN 9780521405997.

Ostrom, Elinor and Charlotte Hess eds. (2007) *Understanding knowledge as a commons: from theory to practice* MIT Press ISBN 9780262516037.

Guy Standing, *The Blue Commons: Rescuing the Economy of the Sea*, Pelican, 2023 ISBN 9780241475881

# Chapter Sixteen
## The Thorny Problem of Population

The subject of population is so controversial that, even if I try to keep it strictly factual, my conclusions will amount to a point of view. The basic fact to be faced is that the human race, like any other animal species, tends to increase its numbers according to the availability of food, and suffer starvation when the food runs out. The dramatic increases in human population have been due to the invention of farming and subsequent "improvements" in how farming is done, along with improved sanitation in cities (drains) and "improvements" in medicine that allow people to live longer [1].

In Britain, where the population has been rising at an average rate of 0.4 percent annually since 1950, some readers might regard the increase as insignificant. But this could be a serious error. Any positive rate of rise can produce an unsustainable population if it continues indefinitely.

Britain thus serves as a useful example; it already needed to import much of its food in the early 1950s. Since then, its large population density and low and decreasing biocapacity indicate an economy far from sustainable [2]. Britain has nevertheless maintained a sufficient level of prosperity since WWII through exporting manufactured goods, consolidating itself as an important financial center, through tourism and, latterly, the exploitation of North Sea oil, this last being a dubious and transitory benefit. A current projection of its population to 2030 can be roughly derived from their government's data for the years 2016-2020, in which the population expansion was nearly linear, increasing an average rate of 387 thousand annually, which would lead to a population of 71 million by 2030. The UK government's projection is somewhat lower, as they also project estimates of net migration. Thinking next of a population *target* for the year 2030, might it not be better set below 2020's 67.2 million, to match the country's declining biocapacity more closely?

I've taken Britain as an opening example of failure to face population realities, since that country has a level of education and sophistication of its population that is high in the scheme of world affairs, and it is an island society, though not in any way isolated. And yet the sustainability factor does not seem to have entered into Britain's social planning. Jared Diamond, in his book *Collapse*, describes an isolated island society that survived 3000 years, through limiting its population to what the island could sustain [3]. By contrast Easter Island failed to do this and that society collapsed.

Human history would suggest that, on the continents, an awareness of needing to limit population never developed as had been necessary in isolated islands, because one could invade neighbors to acquire more territory. This type of action must have begun in the fifth millennium BC [4].

In most countries population is increasing. The populations of some countries in Africa have increased by a factor of five of more in seventy years. According to Worldometers, Nigeria's population increased 2.58 percent from 2919-2020, the highest fractional increase of any country having a population over 100 million [5].

The global population projection in Appendix 2 cries out for halting the current expansion as soon as possible at the lowest possible level: let's say at eight billion. In this way the human race might be spared the appalling threat of population contraction by starvation within thirty years. The problem of feeding more than eight billion people might, however, be overcome, and this would require strong encouragement of sustainable farming.

There is another sufficient reason to halt the population expansion as soon as possible and to begin to decrease human numbers. Human expansion has already crushed the populations of other creatures, most of which have been suffering from declines in their habitats or other depredations that have human cause. Thus, even if our food production can increase to meet human needs 30 years from now, countless species will soon become extinct, and most of the rest will be threatened with extinction.

> The new paradigm calling for life-centered economics therefore demands not merely a halt to human population growth, but a decline.

If we are to survive, the ecosphere must survive, and we are killing it, first by putting carbon dioxide into the ocean (via the air) and second, by making it impossible for the world's interdependent species to flourish, in stark violation of what I have called "The Principle of Life," central to the new paradigm (see Chapter One). Some evidence of the desperate situation of other species is given in Appendix 5.

Evidence for a realistic possibility of an early population maximum was presented at an international roundtable organized by two of my colleagues in 2009 [6]. A demographer speaking on population pointed out that, while the global population had risen by a colossal 75 million souls in 2008, an estimated 80 million pregnancies that same year had been unwanted by the women concerned. Had those women had a choice, there would already have been population stability.

The global population increases have declined yearly from 2013 to 2023, a good start. [Readers are warned against population projections of more than a decade or two, as these become hugely unreliable the further ahead they extend, particularly when modelers making such projections ignore highly probable calamities. Donella Meadows and her co-authors, in their book *Limits to Growth: the 30-Year Update* (Chelsey-Green Publishing, 2004) made no such crucial omission.]


**Policy leading to a stable or reducing world population**

The preparation of a strategy to attain a stable or diminishing world population has largely been the work of very many women, who came together four times between 1975 and 1995 to discuss women's issues, and continue to do so [7]. In addition, the United Nations sponsored a Conference in Cairo in 1994 [8], which crystallized the key points in a policy to restrain population growth. The conference released its four key points in these terms:

1. **Universal education**: Universal primary education in all countries by 2015. Urge countries to provide wider access for women to secondary and higher level education as well as vocational and technical training.

2. **Reduction of infant and child mortality**: Countries should strive to reduce infant and under-5 child mortality rates by one-third or to 50-70 deaths per 1000 by the year 2000. By 2015 all countries should aim to achieve a rate below 35 per 1,000 live births and an under-five mortality rate below 45 per 1,000.

3. **Reduction of maternal mortality**: A reduction by half the 1990 levels by 2000 and half of that by 2015. Disparities in maternal mortality within countries and between geographical regions, socio-economic and ethnic groups should be narrowed.

4. **Access to reproductive and sexual health services including family planning**: Family-planning counseling, pre-natal care, safe delivery and post-natal care, prevention and appropriate treatment of infertility, prevention of abortion and the management of the consequences of abortion, treatment of reproductive tract infections, sexually transmitted diseases and other reproductive health conditions; and education, counseling, as appropriate, on human sexuality, reproductive health and responsible parenthood. Services regarding HIV/AIDS, breast cancer, infertility, and delivery should be made available. Active discouragement of female genital mutilation (FGM).

It is important to recognize that all four points in the published strategy are essential. Item 1 is essential, since in poor countries not all the children in a family have the opportunity of education beyond the earliest grades. Girls are often deprived of further education and never complete school. They are thus confined to tasks at home and tend to be married early and start a new family. Education enables them to seek work and postpone marriage for some years, an important factor in population growth.

The reduction of child mortality is vital. Frequent infant deaths have always been a motive for wanting many children, since otherwise it was too likely that none would survive to adulthood. This applied in distant times within societies that today are prosperous and now have low birth rates and very much lower infant mortality.

The requirement of reduced maternal mortality is an indicator of the needed health services that should, in a just world, be available to all women. Without that, the system must surely be deficient and the parallel requirements more fragile.

The fourth requirement is the most obvious and frequently cited, though it must stand in parallel with the others.

There is also a fifth requirement, not found in the Cairo outcomes, perhaps because it isn't medical. In many poor communities worldwide, children had great importance as those who would care for their parents in their old age. To have only one or two children in such communities lowered very much the likelihood of parents being sustained in their old age. Children were a form of insurance. To remove that need, some form of pension for the aged is required.


**The United Nations Population Fund (UNFPA)**

The UNFPA is key to making good the population policy just described. UNFPA's written objective is to "deliver a world where every pregnancy is wanted, every childbirth is safe and every young person's potential is fulfilled," and it advises countries that this route is the best route to attain sustainable development. UNFPA is also one of the world's largest funders of population data collection. In his book *Common Wealth* (2008) Jeffrey Sachs says of UNFPA that it needs greatly expanded funding; and that it is "the focal point for the effort to stabilize the global population at eight billion by 2015." That objective remains, except that it wasn't reached by 2015.

## Countries having decreasing populations

More than twenty countries now have decreasing populations, though a large fraction of these have populations of only a few million, and the reductions are partly due to emigration because of poor employment opportunities locally. Emigration does not change the global population! Greece and many East European countries fall into this category.

Japan remains the sole example of a nation following its national policy of a slow decline in population. The last 10 years have seen tiny population decreases in Japan tending to a steady decrease of about 0.53 percent annually. What is important here is the widespread social agreement with the national policy.

China has, surprisingly, joined the major countries having attained a decreasing population. The surprise arises from the facts that Chinese population policy is top-down and was, years ago, a limit imposed on families of one child per family. This was much later changed to a maximum of two children per family and more recently relaxed to three children per family. To explain the decrease one needs to suppose: that the birth rate has not increased as might be expected from the relaxation of the policy; and the formerly rapid increase in life expectancy has slowed down.

Four other countries with mid-to-large populations have shown small declines these last four years: Italy, Russia and South Korea and Spain. In all four cases, the declines are contrary to government hopes or policy. Russia has the largest land area by far of any country, so that one can understand that there is room for more people, but the question of biocapacity is always relevant. Russia's largest annual population decline was 0.39 percent, for the year 2020-2021. The declines in Italy were not much larger than those of Russia. The tiny declines in South Korea are due to a very low birth rate, and would be larger if they were not compensated by immigration and/or an increasing expectation of life. All Spain's recent declines have been small. The top-down policies of all four countries are calling for increasing birth rates!

## Age distributions corresponding to long-lived populations

It is well known from demographic studies that populations with low birth rates and high expectation of life have age distributions lacking the very wide base of young people found in countries having high birth rates. This has sometimes given rise to the comment that societies having large percentages of people over 60 will have a shortage of people to serve as care givers for the aged. The evidence is rather that such countries tend also to have a maximum of unemployed among young adults, so overall availability of workers is not in question. There can of course be a shortage of people who *wish* to enter employment in caring for the aged, but, in a fully ecological economy, health will be much improved compared with the present, and we will likely find that being over 65 no longer qualifies as "aged."


## Conclusion

It is essential that global population come to its maximum as soon as possible and then begin a decline. Humanity's global expansion is a major threat to the majority of species with which we share this planet and on whom we depend. A continuing population increase risks widespread human starvation, and will render more difficult the already colossal challenge of addressing climate change, and bringing human society to a sustainable state.

Japan's decline in population is appropriate in view of its high ecological footprint. Population declines are worthy of additional study because of fears that declining population implies economic recession. Such a correlation may or may not occur in a traditional economy, but will not likely be found in an ecological economy where there is a focus on maintaining the good health of the ecosphere.

The author in no way believes that a top-down solution attempting to enforce national population policy can be fully satisfactory. Such implementation can best be brought about through a broadened public understanding, as has occurred in Japan.

**Notes**

1. The quotation marks here indicate merely my skepticism on the merits of certain aspects of modern farming and of modern medicine.

2. www.footprintnetwork.org/resources

3. Jared Diamond *Collapse: How Societies Choose to Fail or Succeed* The Penguin Group 2005.

4. Lack of evidence for war in old Europe prior to 4300 BC is noted in the author's chapter "Democratic Governance: the need for equal representation of women" on page 246 in E Diener and D R Rahtz *Advances in Quality of Life Theory and Research* Kluwer Academic Publishers 2000 pp. 243-60.

5. Worldometers: https://www.worldometers.info/world-population/population-by-country/

6. Roundtable on Food and Population, cohosted by the Global Issues Project (see Appendix 2) and Ryerson University.

7. The United Nations organized four world conferences on women. These took place in Mexico City, 1975, Copenhagen, 1980, Nairobi, 1985 and Beijing, 1995. The last was followed by a series of five-year reviews.

8. The International Conference on Population and Development (ICPD) 1994.

# Chapter Seventeen
## Farming, Food and Human Health

One of the benefits of an ecological economy is that it will be able to cope with the desperate state of farming on small farms in much of the world [1]. Farming is essential, but its continuance on a family scale is uncertain, though some farmers these past seventy years have had considerable financial success by sharing tasks and costly machinery among several medium-sized farms. The case against agribusiness, with its concentration on huge monocultures and excessive use of fertilizers and pesticides, has been made again and again and will not be repeated here. Nevertheless, it is worth taking a second look at the following, often conflicting statements about the prospects of feeding the human race during the forthcoming years. Joel Bourne states that agribusiness is necessary in the short term, as it produces more food per acre than the majority of organic farms [2]. An argument then follows that, if agribusiness' methods were replaced by organic farming, the total food might be insufficient to feed the current population, let alone the growing population of tomorrow [3].

The following three factors counter the foregoing argument. The first, and possibly the most important, is that organic farming optimizes the soil and leaves it as good or better for each subsequent year's crops. Organic nutrition for all would go a long way to improve human health, even if this change alone might lead to diets that are a bit short on calories. The second factor is animal farming, in which raising animals for food requires more acreage for animal feed than the food provided by the slaughtered animals. The most severe case is in raising beef cattle, which require about ten times as much fodder during their short lifetimes as they provide in their meat. The third factor is the use of farmland to produce grain for alcohol fuel, as a supplement to gasoline.

The second of the foregoing factors needs the attention of farmers and governments everywhere, on the road to sustainability.

The third factor, the use of farmland to produce ethanol for fuel, would, however, seem to have no justification whatever. Ethanol production was justified by the false argument that it was neutral in emissions, since the $CO_2$ emitted was compensated by the sequestration by the growth of the grain that provided the fuel. A full examination of this question includes, however, the matter of what would have been grown in place of that grain if the alcohol production had not taken place? Whatever that would have been, the sequestration would have been similar, though not necessarily exactly so, and the emissions would have been avoided.

Grain for alcohol reduces land acreage for growing and reduces the potential of additional natural fertilizer. Growing plants for producing fuel is not neutral, as claimed.

More effective methods for maintaining vehicles powered by gasoline engines on the roads (until they can be replaced by non-emitting power sources) would be: engines of lower power; ride sharing; car shari and stronger reliance on locally produced goods. All of the above are discussed in other chapters.

Diminishing the acreage of farmland used for producing alcohol fuel would increase acreage for farming, especially in the United States, and perhaps reinstate a grain surplus and accelerate conversion of farms to organic status.

The above arguments are presented here as matters for debate at all levels of society, since they affect our future in critical ways. They furthermore have led to the suggestion that conversations are needed among governments, industries' leaders, and the general public.

Organic farming was discussed in Chapter Six, from the standpoint of increasing natural wealth, through putting organic matter into the soil, and we saw that the rate at which organic growing is increasing, at least in North America, is too slow to yield us a sustainable agricultural food system within the next 20-30 crucial years. What the ecological economy can provide are the requirements for improving soil for organic growing, such as additional labor or interest-free loans while the soil quality is being improved and the productivity of the land is still in its growth phase. And this has to be a priority. Organic growing is an important factor in addressing climate change and in attaining sustainability because it will help optimize human health and the condition of the ecosphere, and it increases $CO_2$ sequestration. For further information on organic farming, see Bibliography at the end of this chapter.

## Health

In Chapter Ten there is a brief discussion of food from an industrial point of view applying, *inter alia*, to food processing. Here we can look briefly at the relevance of organic farming, as its future may develop within an ecological economy; will it make a difference? Though the changes will take time, I am convinced that we shall see an improvement in nutritive value of foods, including a restoration of full vitamin and mineral contents to levels experienced prior to agribusiness and its monocultures. It is true that foods having all the benefits referred to here already can be found in health food stores in many developed countries, but these outlets developed because products having the desired qualities could not and cannot yet dominate the major supermarkets, price and availability being important factors.

Next will follow the food price debate. Will people who have become used to food being very cheap [4] be prepared to pay the extra? This cannot be answered now but, if the overall growth of organic production continues, the organic produce will gradually decline in cost as the quality of the soil increases together with output per acre. Subsidizing organic farming in the development phase will also have the effect of reducing the financial cost of products.

Agribusiness is plagued with most complex problems arising, for example, from neonicotinoids in pesticides [5]. A relatively recent example arising from agribusiness is the devastating effect on bees of the use of glyphosate in weed killers. The function of bees in the natural world is of huge importance and cannot be measured in currency. Such are the many externalities that the traditional economy ignores. Glyphosate is also stated to have serious negative effects on human health [6], though this is now contested. Regardless of the outcome of the glyphosate controversy on human health, the use of weed killers in agriculture violates a principle, well-known in organic farming circles, that the products of growth (other than the harvested crops) should be left in place so that the organic matter is recycled within the soil.

One can also ask, "Why the inaction of ministers of health on important questions that, while not presenting immediate dangers, nevertheless affect long-term human health?" Chapter Twelve mentions Maclean's Magazine's May 6, 2014 issue on the dangers of excess sugar, which was entirely well documented and convincing. Nine years later, can anyone see any difference in processed food marketing as a result? Could it be that the needed policy changes would interfere with profit? In an ecological economy, health would come first. And it is doubly important that this should be so, since the challenges faced by the human race are bound to increase these next years.

**Bibliograph**

Andrew Mefferd *The Organic No-Till Farming Revolution* New Society Publishers 2019.

Eliot Coleman *The New Organic Grower* 3rd edition Chelsea Green Publishing 2018.

Gabe Brown *Dirt to Soil* Chelsea Green Publishing 2018.

**Notes**

1. Joel K Bourne *The End of Plenty: the race to feed a crowded world* W W Norton and Company 2015. On pp. 9-11 he gives glimpses of the difficulties of farming in the United States, enough to discourage almost anyone from continuing in his farmer-father's footsteps. The

risks of ruin were simply too great. This book is strongly recommended reading.

2. Joel K Bourne *loc. cit.* Chapter 12 "Organic Agriculture."

3. Joel K Bourne *loc. cit.*

4. For those who don't think supermarket food cheap nowadays (in prosperous, developed countries), they only need to refer back to food prices in, say, the 1950s, which they will find relatively expensive if they do their estimations in currencies corrected for the intervening inflation.

5. https://en.wikipedia.org/wiki/Neonicotinoid

6. See Stephanie Seneff's 2013 video on YouTube: https://www.youtube.com/watch?v=qYC6oyBglZI

# Chapter Eighteen
## Militarism

Among the world's many faulty social structures, military establishments and their relationship with for-profit arms industries stand out as the most dangerous; they could condemn civilization to its end in an hour or so; and they have been sapping planetary resources for decades.

Militarism is a state of mind, born and bred through experience, and very permanent in the minds of those who have acquired it. It can put peace out of reach. Yet it is possible to overcome dominant military influence. More than once, peace has been attained and long preserved in parts of the world where formerly there had been animosity and warfare.

Anatol Rapoport wrote a classic paper for a conference on the defense of Europe in 1985 [1]. An aim of the conference was to draw attention to disarmament of "conventional" weapons, since the peace movement at that time had been strongly focused on nuclear disarmament. Yet, as one of the military experts pointed out at that time, the millions of people killed in armed struggles during the 40 years since the Nagasaki bomb was dropped in 1945 had all been killed by "conventional" weapons, by which he excluded nuclear, chemical and biological weapons. It was also known by then that the vast majority of casualties and deaths in those wars were civilian.

Rapoport's paper is of great generality. In it he says, "None of the time-honored extra-military war aims are worth a war fought with modern weapons of total destruction: not conquest of territory, not trade monopolies, not the imposition of an ideology, not the enslavement of a population. The material costs of modern war must exceed by several orders of magnitude any material benefits." A few pages further on: "Defence? Whom do military establishments defend? There were, to be sure, eras when armies defended their countries from marauders and rapacious invaders... But throughout most of this modern era this has seldom been so. Armies, when on the defensive, have primarily defended themselves, not populations. And populations have been victimized by their own armies as well as the enemy's."

In 1945, the United Nations was created, and this was the most significant global development in international relations since the earliest civilizations. For the first time, national governments everywhere were being invited to treat others as they would like to be treated—the scale of the Golden Rule had become global.

What has changed since then, and what in particular has gone wrong? The list is long, so here's only a partial one. First, the belief in a few countries that they can prevail militarily, and thus fulfill political ambitions to dominate others, none of whom wants to be dominated. Second, the sponsorship of cruel surrogate wars during the long US-USSR confrontation—the Cold War [2]. Third, the failure to disarm multilaterally, which was the purpose of the three Special Sessions of the United Nations (1978, 83, and 88), and much other diplomatic work. Fourth, a host of unjustifiable and destructive military interventions. Fifth, the continued development of more and more new types of weapon, including such as permit internationally illegal, violent action from a distance. Sixth, the failure to distinguish between force, which is sometimes necessary, and violence, which is always to be avoided [3].

Nobody has immediate, practical answers to these dilemmas; otherwise the problems might well have been resolved by now.

## Newer issues

There are also other, newer types of issue in the realm of conflict, of which cyber warfare needs mention. Cyber war has been defined by author Richard Clarke as "actions by a nation state to penetrate another nation's computers or networks for the purposes of causing damage or disruption." [4] One can extend the definition to attack by non-state actors, but then one might prefer to call it cyber crime. Either can be very dangerous, considering the state of armament of some nations, especially those having nuclear weapons. The problem, as always, is: what to do about it? Cyber crime has been with us for many years, though we called it hacking most of the time, and it is still unsolved—we do not see the criminal and haven't learned how to catch him. My view is that the threat of cyber war is yet another message to humanity to cease international rivalry, thereby eliminating cyber war and enabling us to collaborate against cyber crime. The collaboration will be most important because the effects of cyber crime could be as bad as those of cyber war. A regime of prevention must surely be possible and would also protect businesses and private computer systems.

The world of rapid communications now depends almost exclusively on systems established in outer space on near-Earth satellites. Such a system will always be vulnerable, since satellites can be targeted and destroyed, or can suffer an accident in outer space. Though there are at least two countries having technology capable of destroying the orbiting satellites of another state, it is not in the interests of any nation having such technology to use it that way. The threat could, however, arise if a nation so equipped were threatened so seriously with its own destruction that it would act out of desperation. The very complex space system therefore remains vulnerable enough that a parallel communications system—one not dependent on outer space—is really necessary in case of emergency. These matters are independent of whether an ecological economy is in place, but the ecological economy requires a regime of peace, as does the human race if it wants to come out of its present predicaments alive and well; and peace is a huge step forward toward reducing the threats just discussed.

It had been noted c.2003, by Project Ploughshares, Canada's major peace research institute, that wars between nations were on the decline, and that the remaining armed conflicts, which were internal national conflicts, became more and more complex in their composition of rival groups. The increasing complexity is not easy to deal with, but surely a more collaborative international climate will ease such problems. The armed struggles, in addition to all the other depredations of conflict, are very troublesome in displacing people, as the UN Commissioner for Refugees' budget tells us, since it exceeded $9bn USD in 2021, and was similar in 2022. I therefore conclude this section with a few points and questions on some of the world's unresolved conflicts. The attack on Afghanistan, when the Taliban were in control, failed in the sense that the Taliban continued fighting when their invaders had gotten tired of that conflict. The overly violent British-American invasion of Iraq did huge harm but has not brought about a general stability there, and it gave birth to ISIS, which in turn made a resolution of the Syrian crisis much more painful, and has given rise to especially difficult situations in Africa.

Does the war perpetrated by Saudi Arabia against Yemen have any justification? Do the Kurds have to be military targets of aggression in the several countries in which they live? These last examples illustrate stronger nations attacking weaker neighbors or ethnic groups within their boundaries in overpopulated areas of the world.

Lastly, a satisfactory end to the war in the Ukraine can only be one that is negotiated, while the escalating war of Israel against Palestinians within the territory Israel controls or elsewhere can only retard human progress in addressing its greatest threats.

If there is a solution to any such aggression, it requires the recognition by relevant leaders and their cabinets that their policies are not working. The Nationalist Party of South Africa stopped its apartheid policy when one of its leaders recognized that apartheid was not working. Thirty years earlier, you could never have convinced any member of the Nationalist Party that their apartheid policy could fail.

The above list barely touches upon the ways in which militaristic policies fail; and in which policies to control others fail.

Evidence that national military policies are failing comes from the failure to address climate change, the huge numbers of refugees, the decline of species, the dying ocean, and the failure to create sustainable societies [5]. This is because all major issues are interrelated, and **every resource put into military violence in this over-armed world adds emphasis to the failures**.

The new phrase, the redeeming principle is *international cooperation.*

## Notes

1. Anatol Rapoport "Whose Security does Defence defend?" in *Defending Europe: Options for Security* Taylor and Francis 1986 pp. 271-80.

2. The Cold War between the USA and its allies and the Soviet Union lasted for four decades starting soon after the defeat of Germany in 1945. It got its name from the fact that there was no military aggression between the two sides during all those years, but the many threatening confrontations continued past the 1970s and were heightened to a crisis by the election of Ronald Reagan as President of the United States (November 1979), the failure of the USA to sign the long-awaited treaty on nuclear arms limitation (SALT 2), the Soviet invasion of Afghanistan (late December 1979), and the US decision the same year to target Soviet Missile silos instead of cities with their intercontinental missiles, which was interpreted in the USSR as a move to make possible a US nuclear first strike. Although there was no direct, violent aggression US-USSR, both sides armed and supported different parties in other violent conflicts, such as the first part of the civil war in Angola (1975-91).

3. The distinction is emphasized in Ely Culbertson's *Total Peace* Doubleday Doran and Company 1943.

4. Richard A Clarke *Cyber War* Harper Collins.

5. *Global Footprint News* also Mathis Wackernagel and Bert Beyers *Ecological Footprint: Managing Our Biocapacity Budget* New Society Publishers 2019.

# Chapter Nineteen
## Inequalities: Income and Power

Inequality has most often been presented in terms of the incomes of the best-off and worst-off individuals in a given society. Economists sometimes assess inequality by computing the average income in each income decile of a given population; a simple measure of inequality then becomes the ratio of averages of the top and bottom deciles.

This type of inequality grew slightly in the 1970s, and more rapidly since then, especially in the United States and Canada. The current trend could lead eventually to the appalling prospect of unnecessary human poverty for the great majority of people.

Much has been written on inequality of incomes by Thomas Piketty [1], coauthors Richard Wilkinson and Kate Pickett [2], and Joseph Stiglitz [3]. Stiglitz explains the social inequalities in terms of politics: the failure of democracy. If the rich can influence policy so that they receive an increasing share of the pie, this produces more and more inequality. Inequality is surely unjust, but is it eroding the law? Clearly, Stiglitz thinks it is in the USA.

Piketty uses the statistics of income, salary, benefits, salary deductions and all taxes to show that the inequalities are roughly proportional to salary inequalities in Europe, the USA, and Canada. He is in favor of reducing inequalities and proposes a system of redistribution through taxation. He defines what he calls *taux effectifs marginaux* (effective marginal rates), which can be applied to salaries, additional benefits, salary deductions and taxes, so as to compute how much someone gains in net finances by climbing out of a lower salary group to a higher. He claims that the lowest salary decile gains the least because of stiff deductions and/or loss of benefits, and says that governments would do well to make this situation less discouraging.

Wilkinson and Pickett provide many data showing some correlation (but nowhere strong correlation) between the rich-poor income gap and other undesirable social features, but their strength is in their various conclusions. They and Piketty agree that the central problem is salary spread between the richest and poorest of the employed, which is too great.

The three books span 800 pages, with over 1000 references and a bibliography of over 120 books, but the rich-poor gap continues to increase. Let's therefore have a fresh look at the problem, its historical context, how the present inequality was so easily achieved, and what could now be done about it.

A huge historical error of Western civilization was to largely deregulate banks [4] while allowing continuance of: profit-making as the sole objective of corporations, including banks; and other conditions described below. For many years, major corporations had already shown great skill at bargaining for good conditions, including subsidies and low taxes, when they wanted to start manufacturing. Most countries wanted manufacturing set up within their territory, because of the employment created and new taxes (however modest), so they agreed to the conditions. The process is competitive in that other countries also want the manufacturing within their jurisdiction, and the "contract" goes to the lowest bidder—the jurisdiction that offers the most and wants the least in tax. It became a race to the bottom, with wealthy corporations paying as little as seven percent tax on huge profits. Tax avoidance is further exacerbated by tax havens. The subject of tax havens is complex, and I draw attention here to the type of tax haven made possible by a country that has set up a legal process through which a corporation can claim to have established plant and/or head offices there, while those physical entities may not be found there at all. Such conditions accentuate the continuing widening distribution of individual wealth.

This whole picture was preventable and can be reversed.

Containing this kind of corporate behavior requires the heads of states to agree on terms that they require of businesses, and to persist in policies that would effectively eliminate tax havens. Also, there will likely have to be severe penalties for infringement of such agreements. The current situation arose because governments saw each other as in competition, and were thus exploitable, whereas they need to be cooperating on the road to prosperity—world, not just local prosperity—something that is essential in the ecological economy.

At the same time, corporate profit is a general good and is needed globally if pensions are to be provided where they are needed, a continually changing picture as life expectancy increases globally, as it has long been doing. Therefore a new method of taxing corporations is called for, one that incorporates thresholds as in personal income taxation, and justly takes into account corporate size—see Chapter Seven, end of first section.

Returning now briefly to inequality, what might be an acceptable goal? Most employees in most occupations earn less than one *Sal*, where the Sal is a top annual salary for someone in government or public life or any of the bureaucracies; one might think of it for convenience as the President's (or the Prime Minister's) annual salary. Maybe the world could live with a system in which the Sal was twelve times the minimum yearly wage based upon a 36-hour week, and nobody had more annual spending income than a few Sal [5].

The inequality problem stems from the fact that the corporate wealthy have managed to create a new class of super-rich, analogous to but not at all resembling the aristocracy of the nineteenth century. The Sal becomes a pittance in this class. The new aristocracy uses its power to increase its monetary wealth both intelligently and mindlessly: intelligently, because it knows very well how to increase that monetary wealth, and because some corporations are doing most admirable things in this world; mindlessly, because other corporations have no regard for health as broadly discussed in this book, and some are contributing hugely to what could very soon become an irreversible climate disaster.

To restore the needed balance of power between governments, collectively, and corporations, the former will have to collaborate to agree on a new *Carta Magna* of terms for the new rich, the reverse of the process in 1215, when it was the ruler who had to be held in check by the aristocracy [6]. In so doing, governments will need to be prepared (and if necessary legislate) to remove corporate charters in cases of serious environmental damage. Simultaneously many governments will have to learn to base policy on evidence, rather than whim. Addressing climate change and attaining a sustainable civilization will become easier once this is accomplished.

The rest is detail, though the details are important. Some of it will be in the *Carta Magna*, more to follow later.

It seems likely that Monsieur Bruno Le Maire, France's Finance Minister since 2017, already set the ball rolling through his tax on digital enterprises. He said that several European countries had followed suit by setting a similar tax [7].

Since the G7 meeting, 11-13 June 2021, 130 nations have made a great step forward in the same direction [8].

**Notes**

1. Thomas Piketty *L'économie des inégalités* seventh edition Editions la Découverte 2015. This book exists in an English translation, *The Economics of Inequality* (2015).

2. Richard Wilkinson and Kate Pickett *The Spirit Level: Why Equality is Better for Everyone* Penguin 2010.

3. Joseph E Stiglitz *The Price of Inequality: how today's divided society endangers our future* W W Norton and Company 2012.

4. https://en.wikipedia.org/wiki/Big_Bang_(financial_markets)

5. Very large incomes or earnings will not be avoidable, unless the mean-spirited want to deny successful and remarkable people, whose incomes are surely in excess of a few Sal, the pleasure of using their wealth constructively. Issues of this kind can be handled through investment directives, which, in the ecological economy, might include some special requirements.

6. This concept is essential to the ecological economy, to bring us to a sustainable existence and to do it fast enough to avoid the climate transition, and the continuing increase in inequality.

7. Speech made by M. Le Maire at the TaxCOOP2020 conference, 16 October 2020.

8. *Le Devoir*, B5, 2 July 2021: Marie Heuclin of Agence France-Presse claimed a "historic day for the OECD," which had concluded an agreement among 130 nations on a new system of corporate taxation that will demand a minimum of 15 percent from multinationals. According to Bruno Le Maire this fiscal agreement is the most important one of the last hundred years. See also: OECD taxation of Multinational Corporations (online): "Tax Incentives and the Global Minimum Corporate Tax," 6 Oct. 2022.

# Chapter Twenty

## Using New Indices of Wealth and Prosperity

There are two traditional issues here. One is the familiar list of objections to GDP (gross domestic product) as an indicator of general economic prosperity, and the other is the need for an index of human wellbeing. Both are discussed below. However, it is important to note that an index intended to measure human prosperity may merely give us an average that hides profound economic misery resulting from unequal distribution of economic goods. A truly meaningful index in an ecological economy would therefore have to be more than a measure of averages, and I do not claim it can be done with a single parameter. For example, an index of incomes for a given population would at least need to show the average income and also the spread in incomes

In the ecological economy we shall also need indices of resource wealth and of the state of living things on this planet.

**Fiscal indices**

The fiscal index used everywhere at present is the gross domestic product. Investopedia gives the following formula for calculating GDP:

$$GDP = C + G + I + NX$$

where C is private consumer spending, which includes all manner of enterprises, G is the sum of spending by governments, I is the sum of the country's investment, including businesses' capital expenditures, and NX is the total of exports minus imports, in fiscal terms. Omitted from the GDP formula are trades between family members or friends, the underground economy, which includes all other unreported trading, and much of the trading that uses private currencies and cryptocurrencies.

The GDP index is nevertheless considered important as a measure of relative prosperity, both by governments and by people in commerce, but it has been hugely criticized in that it is calculated without regard to how or why the expenditures were made. There are dozens of examples of objections to GDP [1]; I will only mention two. When disaster hits a country, and huge sums must be spent to restore capital assets, and there may also be great losses of natural wealth, GDP usually rises, because it measures the costs of the repairs and reconstruction, and it ignores any loss of natural and built wealth. Again, though its aim is to indicate prosperity, it has nothing to say about the state of contentment of the people. Consumerism will increase GDP, but may not give any increase in human happiness, and it can cause considerable pollution of the environment.

A claimed improvement on GDP is the net domestic product, which subtracts depreciation of produced assets from the GDP formula, and therefore represents more accurately the fiscal aspect of prosperity. But net domestic product has not caught on; all governments and economists continue to quote GDP, which hides so many important details. The net domestic product would also hide all of those details except depreciation and built-capital losses due to neglect or disasters.

## An index of human wellbeing

In Daly and Cobb's book *For the Common Good* (1989) there is an Appendix on an index of economic welfare. Max-Neef mentions [2], however, that their index has morphed into the Genuine Progress Index (GPI). The GPI, now widely called the Genuine Progress Indicator, is discussed in Nickerson's book, already cited [3], and elsewhere. Guardian Sustainable Business [4] states that 20 US states have already adopted the Genuine Progress Indicator as a substitute for GDP. In 2012, Vermont was the first state to pass into law this new metric for measuring economic prosperity. The difference between GDP and GPI is that GPI subtracts many negative factors from the GDP, such as assessed damage to the health of the ecosphere, reduced built wealth, and damages to the social system itself. One of the subtracted factors in determining the GPI comes from inequality. Altogether, there are 26 elements combined in the GPI.

GPI needs to increase as long as there is abject poverty or dire poverty, but a point must come soon enough in the global future when the totals of GDP and GPI for all countries cease to rise and begin to decline in sync with the decline of human population.

There are many other indicators of wellbeing, for example, the United Nations' Human Development Index, and the 20-odd OECD indicators, but the GPI was chosen for present purposes, as combining many into one that might counteract the deficiencies of the GDP.

## Wealth measurement in an ecological economy

The concentration on purely fiscal matters repeatedly reveals failures of the traditional economy. This does not mean that financial accounting will cease in an ecological economy; it will likely be little changed. The requirements in an ecological economy will, however, be to measure and keep track of capital resources, including natural resources. This is already done for forest lumber in some jurisdictions, and is important. But forest resources are also closely tied to human development; and forest provides much habitat for other species.

Fish stocks and species of all sorts will be important, since they are mostly threatened today or in steep decline. Environmental information is often found in the hands of nongovernmental organizations, and it remains to be seen what kind of relationships will develop between such organizations and the emancipated future governments that will be emerging from their traditional roles into the new era of a full life.

An idea of natural wealth accounting at government level can be obtained from the work of NRTEE [5].

The science of measurement of resources and their movement and effects due to international trade was already well advanced early in the first decade of the 21$^{st}$ century. For example, in 2007 Karen Turner et al. published a major two-part paper examining the global impact of regional consumption [6]. This is very complex material; the reference is given here to emphasize the work that ecological economists are already doing in preparation for a new economy.

## The growth factor

It might appear at first sight that GPI is "the" solution to measurement of prosperity within an ecological economy. It is certainly looking good, as it represents a huge advance beyond GDP, but we must be cautious, because the growth element, that is, the belief that "growth is good *per se*" persists in the jurisdictions using the GPI. Thus, until now, GPI remains a creature of the traditional system, albeit a system trying to reform itself.

Tim Jackson [7] and Peter Victor [8] have separately and jointly done splendid pioneer work to convince people in business that economic growth is not a necessary feature of a healthy economy. Herman Daly, now deceased, was also prominent in this matter [9]. These authors' theme is a prologue to setting up an ecological economy.

## Notes

1. Mike Nickerson's *Life, Money and Illusion* 2006 and 2009 has over 20 references to GDP, almost all highly negative.

2. Philip B Smith and Manfred Max-Neef *Economics unmasked* Green Books 2011 Chapter 10 (threshold hypothesis).

3. Mike Nickerson *loc. cit.* pp. 223-25. Nickerson and colleagues have been pursuing the notion of a genuine progress index (GPI) these many years, which reached the stage of a parliamentary motion in Ottawa, which passed with a large majority in 2003, but was not acted upon by government.

4. https://www.theguardian.com/sustainable-business/2014/sep/23

5. National Roundtable on the Environment and the Economy (NRTEE) *Environment and Sustainable Development Indicators for Canada* Renouf Publishing Ltd 2003 ISBN 1-894737-06-7.

6. Karen Turner M Lenzen T Wiedmann & J Barrett (2007) "Examining the global environmental impact of regional consumption activities—Part 1: A technical note on combining input-output and ecological footprint analysis", *Ecological Economics* **62** (1) pp. 37-44; Part 2: "Review of input–output models for the assessment of environmental impacts embodied in trade" T Wiedmann et al. Elsevier c. 2007, available at www.sciencedirect.com

7. Tim Jackson *Prosperity Without Growth: Economics for a Finite Planet* 2nd edition Routledge 2016.

8. Peter Victor *Managing Without Growth: Slower by Design, Not Disaster* Edward Elgar Publishing second edition 2019.

9. Herman E Daly *From Uneconomic Growth to a Steady-State Economy* Edward Elgar Publishing 2014.

# Chapter Twenty-One
## China

China and India account for 35 percent of the world's human population and both are fast developing economically. While India's development is at a comparatively early stage, China's has leaped forward, reducing poverty by a huge factor in under 41 years, and China continues to develop its industries and increase its export business. China's recent history and its status as an industrial colossus pose two vital questions for the world. The first: can China reduce its immense annual emissions of greenhouse gases (ghgs) in time to allow the possibility of forestalling a climate catastrophe? China is of course not alone in the matter of having to reduce its emissions, but many other nations, the USA, for example, could reduce theirs enough, though the will to do so there has been missing in the corridors of power. In China's case, it is equally true that the political will must be present, but could it be done technically speaking?

The second question is this: can developing countries reduce poverty as China has done without increasing their ghg emissions the way China did? This question is of vital importance and is far from being resolved, but a satisfactory solution could surely be realized, given enough international cooperation.


**China's booming economy**

China began its remarkable build-up of civil industry in 1978, soon after the death of Mao Tse Tung, under the growing influence of politician Deng Xiaoping. Between then and now, the economy has grown at an astonishing pace, recently becoming the world's largest industrial economy, as measured by GDP, the indicator that China chose to use. From 2007-2014 it achieved a stunning growth rate of over 15 percent annually, though dropping to about 6.9 percent (or less) in 2015 [1], and continuing since then at lower levels that have been different in different reports! Coal made such rapid development possible, since China had coal deposits, and coal-burning power stations are much more rapidly built and brought into operation than most other alternatives.

## Poverty elimination

The growth rapidly brought the population out of poverty—the lot of over half a billion rural Chinese in 1978—leaving fewer than 25 million in poverty in 2017. This great achievement is reflected in the Human Development Index (HDI) for China, which rose steadily from about 0.42 in 1980 to 0.718 in 2010, about the world average, and then more slowly until it reached 0.752 in 2018 and 0.768 in 2022.

## Fuelling China's electrical needs

In addition to coal burning, China also has the world's largest output of hydroelectric power, and has rapidly developed photovoltaic, wind and nuclear power. Its wind power capacity is already large, but it has the potential to increase that output by more than a factor of two.

By 2017, with some coal-fired power stations operating at only 44 percent of full capacity, and people protesting against the excessive air pollution in their cities, permission for constructing new coal-fired plant was rarely given.

Reliable data enabled me in 2017 to make rough projections of electrical supplies to the year 2020, which ended a five-year plan. The numbers are shown in the 2020 column of table 21.1. The electrical output from coal is colossal at 1100 GWe (gigawatt electrical; giga = billion) and the other numbers are all large compared with what one would find in other jurisdictions. For wind and photovoltaic (PV) energy conversion, my sources gave only the installed capacities, so I had to estimate the likely electrical outputs. Though the PV output is the lowest, the progress in solar PV in China is impressive. The solar intensity at the Earth's surface is barely 1 kW/m$^2$, and the efficiency of conversion of solar to electric power is lower than 30 percent, so we need at least 3.3 square meters of panels to produce 1 kW at noon on a sunny day. But the average sunshine intensity is only one third of this; therefore the 40 GWe average in table 21.1 requires a noon maximum of over 130 GWe. The installation requires at least 130 X 3.3 = 430 square km of panels!

## Greenhouse gas emissions

In 2015, China's emissions amounted to 10.6 GT (gigatonnes) of carbon dioxide, or 27 percent of the world's huge total, while its population numbered under 18 percent of the global total. Where is this headed? By 2015, the rate of growth of China's emissions had slowed but the emissions themselves did not look likely to peak until 2029 [2], at which time the output could be close to 13 Gt per annum, implying a continuing huge $CO_2$ output until well after that date. These factors called for numerical estimates—table 21.1—and added emphasis to recommendations in Chapter Twenty-Two under the subheading Climate change.

## Further projections of China's energy mix

This section presents table 21.1, which is only intended to illustrate a possible future in electrical supply. Projections to 2030 are subject to major uncertainties in the continued growth of some of the energy sources. For similar reasons, projections beyond 2030 contain much guesswork, and the uncertainties in the estimates tabulated are inevitably large. In 2017 it was necessary to project a huge continuing output from coal-burning power plants to 2020, and a remaining output almost half as large by 2030. Then a new policy was announced and published in *Paris-Match*, 2 December 2018, that China planned to produce 500 GWe average of solar power by 2030, an almost unimaginably huge increase in what had been planned previously. When an undertaking as immense as this is announced, there are bound to be skeptics who dismiss the stated objective as unattainable, or declare that it will not happen for political reasons. This chapter is primarily based, however, on Chinese reports, and fig.21.1 is thus based on Chinese information, not Western skepticism, though I was obliged to postulate a possible addition of 80 GWe to their grid from solar concentration by 2050, to bring their coal-fired output to zero by that date, an important objective. Note that Table 21.1 retains a component of gas-fired production of electric power in 2050, in keeping with a declaration by President Xi Jinping in September 2020 at the United Nations that China would achieve carbon neutrality by 2060.

Table 21.1
Electrical projections to 2050, in GWe

| Year | 2020 | 2030 | 2050 |
|---|---|---|---|
| Coal-fired | 1,100 | 500 ? | 0 ? |
| Gas-fired | 110 | 220 ? | 220 ? |
| Hydroelectric | 340 | 340 | 340 |
| Wind | 50 | 80 ? | 200 ? |
| Solar PV | 40 | 500 | 500 ? |
| Solar concentration | 0 | 0 ? | 80 ? |
| Nuclear | 50 | 80 | 240 |
| Total | 1,690 | 1,720 ? | 1,580 ? |
| Renewable subtotal | 430 | 1.000 ? | 1,120 ? |

The question marks in table 21.1 indicate the less certain estimates or guesswork, the other numbers being justifiable from present knowledge. All numbers in the table have been rounded to the nearest 10 GWe. The 200 GWe for wind power in 2050, a pure guess, comes from less than half China's exploitable wind capacity (2,380 GW), which, converted at 22 percent would give an electrical output of 520 GWe. Solar PV power could grow between 2030 and 2050, though this has not been assumed here. What has been assumed is that China will follow a path of developing solar concentration, not by the tower method, which is known to be expensive, but rather, with rotatable Fresnel lenses, which

134

promise to be much cheaper. Solar concentration has the great advantage of providing electrical power continuously, since the intense heat produced can be stored for use at night in small stones underground. The numbers for nuclear power are based upon installed capacities multiplied by optimistic fractional average power outputs for such installations, while the installed capacities are based on building plans to 2030. Should China develop its maximum wind capacity, ghg emissions in electricity production could be reduced to zero by 2050, assuming a total power generation no higher than about 1600 GWe.

The reduced total electrical output assumed in table 21.1 would stem from increasing efficiency in electrical use over the intervening years, and the expectation of a declining population. For China's population trend, see Chapter Sixteen, Countries having decreasing populations.

One can forecast from trends these last few years that electrical production will peak at or before 2030, but that its subsequent decline will be slow. These results are very rough, but we are talking of a 30-year forward look, which is inevitably subject to major uncertainty.


## Is China's economy fully ecological?

The type of economy China has chosen doesn't fit any standard picture. It follows the path of a very successful traditional economy, with important differences. It has brought the great mass of the population out of poverty, and has successfully tackled major projects in renewable energy while arguing the need to preserve its environment. It also would appear to have embraced the concept of preserving a healthy environment globally, except for its huge use of coal and its exports of obsolete coal-burning technology. China is now paying the price for its coal-powered successes through medical costs arising from the pollution of city air, and the huge challenge to eliminate ghg emissions from fossil fuels. It is also taking the risks that accompany the adoption of nuclear power, a Faustian bargain. All in all, China is part way to becoming an ecological economy, but we must look at the growth question.

China's GDP growth, at least to 2010, was necessary to bring the great majority of people out of poverty, and there could be some need for more growth to eliminate poverty entirely. However, a six percent annual growth of GDP would double the economy in only 17 years! Since the population may already have peaked (see Chapter Sixteen), the need for GDP growth must already be small.

The Chinese emphasis on growth, however, mimics the traditional belief that growth is good *per se*, and may thus be an example of what Herman Daly called *growthmania* [3], or what Richard Douthwaite called *growth imperative* [4]. Douthwaite studied England's economy from the 18th century up to 1910 and noticed that the spurts of intensive growth, when industry was already well developed, enriched the capitalists but didn't benefit the labor they employed. By contrast, the work force tended to benefit more from the periods of slow growth. Clearly, China's present growth rate benefits many entrepreneurs but, might the work force do better in a slower-growth mode? This is not to say that China's economy is a historical cycle following England's past mode, but merely that it could be useful to see whether the lot of workers in China is in any way related to the growth rate. The ecological economist will accept the eventual degrowth of an economy, as the population subsides. Degrowth, however, is likely not in anyone's mind in today's China.

Another feature of China's economy is the official attitude to employment. China's annual entry into the job market includes about 15 million people who have completed advanced academic or technical studies. The regime wants to see them usefully employed. This drives further economic expansion. The nature of the economy can be assessed from the selection of employment. If all enter into profit-oriented enterprises, then the approach is traditional (or neoliberal); if enough are working to increase natural wealth and other conditions of humanity and of the ecosphere, then it suggests the ecological option.

China's economy must already be close to the point where most of the increase in production must be exported. It is a most successful exporter, partly because it controls its exchange rate to make sales favorable and maintains (seen from the rest of the world) a low minimum wage. However, the very success of those exports can increase unemployment elsewhere. In the 1980s, the late Eric Kierans, a former Minister of Finance in Canada, remarked that all nations would love to export their unemployment [5]. He was referring precisely to this phenomenon we can see in China's future, though it may be that no one in China has yet seen it in that light. Because modern production methods can produce all the goods that people need with a small fraction of the world's total workforce, maintaining one's own people employed *industrially* and exporting very extensively in fact implies creating unemployment elsewhere. This is one of the reasons for general adoption of an ecological economy, since the job market will then include employment in ecological projects.

Chinese commercial success has been assisted by hoarding gold and US currency, as well as lending huge sums to the U.S. Government. This success was aided and abetted by entrepreneurs from Western civilization who fell for the short-term benefit to themselves of producing abroad where labor was cheap. China has succeeded better at keeping production at home than the English during the heyday of their colonial empire. Some Chinese documents reveal their writers' thinking on keeping production local [2,6].

**Postscript**

Questions remain. Will China succeed in greening its energy supplies through existing technology sufficiently to make the path to zero emissions evident by 2050? Table 21.1 suggests that China's ghg emissions from the electrical generation could be reduced to zero and likely will have declined about 90 percent by 2050. An important factor is that few coal-burning power stations had been built since 2015. However, a recent announcement of huge increases in coal-burning power stations approved in 2022 could change all that—**see Afterword, third page**. China's geothermal energy program continued and accounted for roughly 1 percent of all energy production in 2020 [7]. China also has an electrical generation program using the tower method of solar concentration. The untried method of solar concentration using Fresnel lenses has been studied by professional inventor J M J Varga, who claims it will be very much cheaper than the tower method [8]. Solar concentration is best suited to hot climates where the average solar heat flux is greatest.

**Notes**

1. World Bank data.
Gordon Chang, however, argues that China's growth rate dropped to about 1 percent in 2015:
https://www.forbes.com/sites/gordonchang/2016/01/17/chinas-economy-grew-about-1-in-2015/#31c035252c6d

2. Xinhua News Agency *Green China Green Economy* 2016. The estimate of 5.4 percent annual increases in greenhouse gas emissions is elsewhere stated to be 3.3 percent, and these numbers are hard to verify, because they depend on small differences between large numbers having appreciable uncertainties. It is also important to recognize from Chinese data that when they say "emissions are down by such and such percent by comparison with 2005," it means that the increase in emissions was less than the increase in GDP by that percentage!

3. Herman E Daly *From Uneconomic Growth to a Steady-State Economy* Edward Elgar 2014.

4. Richard Douthwaite *The Growth Illusion* Council Oak Books 1993.

5. The Hon. Eric Kierans, 1987, private communication on the question of unemployment in a work in progress of his at that time.

6. Nuclear Power in China: http://www.world-nuclear.org/information-library/country-profiles/countries-a-f/china-nuclear-power.aspx

7. https://www.thinkgeoenergy.com/china-pushing-ambitious-geothermal-heating-goals-for-2020/

8. J M J Varga, former president of Crosrol Ltd. UK, private communication c.2014-2021.

# Chapter Twenty-Two

## Recommendations

Each recommendation is numbered according to its group, and the groups are indicated by means of the subtitles below. The first recommendation lies at the heart of ecological economics.

This edition follows the numbering of recommendations used in previous editions of this book.

### General recommendation

1. That the United Nations Economic and Social Council prepare a Declaration, to be signed by all UN member nations, to the effect that world economic affairs both within and among nations shall henceforth be conducted with the health and wellbeing of the ecosphere and of humanity as the overriding priority for the future of this planet.

Note 1. The intention implicit in this recommendation is that its objective would become a part of human consciousness. See the discussion of the new paradigm in Chapter One.

### Fiscal preparations

2. That governments make preparations to finance at nominal interest the task of addressing climate change and setting up a sustainable economy.

2b. That the BIS rule that forbids national banks from issuing loans at "nominal" interest be set aside.

2c. That wealthy nations cooperatively provide resources, technology, know-how and, where necessary, funds, to assist poorer nations in addressing climate change.

Note 2c This recommendation could be assisted through the setting up of think tanks within existing institutes that would propose relevant projects.

**Full employment**

3. That all nations forthwith develop full employment policies by establishing wealth-creating projects such as those suggested in Chapter Six; and implement a full employment policy without delay.

3a. That in fulfilling the objectives of recommendation 3, project managers/committees/etc. prioritize full employment for youth, especially in the age group 18-30, and employment outside college terms for those who are in post-secondary education or training.


**Planning**

4. That all governments, especially national governments and state or provincial governments in geographically large jurisdictions, that do not have high-level roundtables with the mandate to look ahead 30 years, create such roundtable(s) without delay. See last part of Chapter Ten: a study of Ontario.

Note 4. This recommendation arose from the conspicuous absence of such a roundtable among the very numerous roundtables of the Ontario Government c.2014, notwithstanding many difficulties facing that government, for example, in energy planning.

4a. That such roundtables be provided with fully adequate modeling services.

Note 4a. The wording of this recommendation arises from evidence of inadequate approaches to modeling.

4b. That in addition to pursuing studies demanded by its respective government, a roundtable would be free to investigate problems it deems advisable and necessary.

4c. That planning for cities by city governments follow the precepts of 4 through 4b where practicable, with attention to recent strategies for the development of sustainable neighborhoods within cities.

4d. That large-scale planning in future include building of new cities in agriculturally least fertile regions.

**Taxation and government-corporate relations**

5. That taxes on services and on value-added be abolished, and replaced by taxes on primary resources: non-renewable ores; and trees. See last part of Chapter Nine.

5a. That priority be accorded to national and international efforts on the measures suggested in Chapters Seven and Nineteen on reducing income inequity, and on the need for rational and fair corporate taxation, for which a just international code is needed.

5b. That nations together form and pursue a joint policy of plugging tax loopholes.

Note 5b. This follows principles that taxes should be paid predominantly by those who can easily afford to do so, and that everyone should contribute their fair share of the tax burden.

5c. That tax-exempt business expenses everywhere be reviewed to introduce stricter limits, where exemptions amount to loopholes.

Note 5c. This is necessary because people working for businesses are strongly favored in many jurisdictions within the traditional economic system compared with those not so employed—a systemic injustice.

5d. That business/corporate profits be subject to *no fewer tax thresholds* as are present in personal income tax systems, and that corporate taxation be rationalized on a per employee basis. See Chapter Seven.

5e. That corporate law everywhere be changed to prevent "hostile" takeovers of businesses.

Note 5e. This recommendation follows from evidence that such takeovers benefit only very few individuals and can and often do have negative effects on the business taken over.

5h. That studies be undertaken in all jurisdictions having stock markets, to evaluate the factors necessary to keep the fraction of money in circulation in the tertiary economy to a modest and more-or-less constant fraction of the total, and to introduce taxation or other rules to bring about the desired result. See Chapters Two and Four.

5i. Because taxation is usually a considerable burden on taxpayers, and in view of the forthcoming financial needs of governments (national or federal) to address climate change, that governments review their internal expenditures with a view to reducing them.

## Climate change

6. That governments, industries, institutions and individuals move forward on climate change initiatives without waiting for others to follow their lead in addressing that threat. See last section, Chapter Eight.

6a. That everyone encourage and take part in much-needed *conversations* among government, industries, institutions, non-governmental organizations, and individuals on how to accelerate the reductions of fossil-fuel burning, sector by economic sector, so as to bring these emissions to zero.

Note 6a. This recommendation follows from the normally longer-term planning of industries than is usually found in government—the duration of a parliament—typically four years. Industries need to know what will be legally expected of them so as to plan what they can supply that will satisfy customers and will use emissions-free technology.

6b. That all shall encourage governments to bring fossil-fuel burning rapidly to zero through direct policy, where the technology to do so already exists. See Chapter Eight, section CanESS.

6c. That governments cease from subsidizing corporations in the fossil-fuel sectors and instead encourage development in other fields, where necessary offering subsidies to make the change.

6d. That in jurisdictions where there is currently manufacture of engines for long-range aircraft or ocean-going ships, additional research and development should be undertaken toward emissions-free propulsion, with a view to having some such propulsion in service for air and ocean transport by 2035, and full implementation of such emissions-free propulsion by 2050. See Chapter Eleven.

6e. That an essential added focus on the reabsorption of carbon from the atmosphere be brought into the public discussion, and to the attention of governments. See Chapter Six and recommendation 7.

6f. That governments take note of the Rodale Institute's claim that regenerative farming worldwide could sequester as much $CO_2$ as the human race is putting into the atmosphere annually, and encourage plans to convert farms to "organic" at rates that will bring about 70 percent of all farms globally by the year 2040. See also recommendation 7.

6g. That research and development of emissions-free manufacture of cement be greatly accelerated, where necessary through subsidies.


**Wealth creation**

7. That each national government create and fund without delay a special organization (or organizations) that would plan and carry out projects to increase natural wealth in farmlands and forest, and reduce and eliminate pollution of rivers and lakes. See Chapter Six.

Note 7. This recommendation replaces 7, 7a, 7b and 7f in earlier editions of this book. Implicitly, this recommendation would pursue, *inter alia*, the goal of increasing total acreages of organic farms. The proposed new organizations are urgently needed, since the goals are long-term and will take many years to fulfill, even to a modest degree. The projects envisaged in this recommendation will also play an important role in maintaining full employment during the transition to zero emissions and for a long time afterwards. See Chapter Six.

7d. That governments worldwide generously support current efforts to stem the advance of the Sahara Desert in Africa. See Chapter Six, The Great Green Wall of Trees to Halt the Sahara, and htpps://pulitzercenter.org/projects/africa-senegal-great-green-wall-trees-sahara-desert-sahel

7e. That international efforts be initiated and energetically pursued to address the protection of the sea bed, and its possible inclusion as part of the global commons. See Chapter Fifteen.

## Businesses

10. For all those who live in a jurisdiction that doesn't have benefit corporations or their equivalent, to lobby for legislation that will open that legal channel. See Chapter Thirteen.

10a. Encourage articles in the press about the advantages of benefit corporations.

## Energy conservation

12. That municipal governments explore and pursue strategies that would reduce the baseload.

Note 12. The baseload is here defined as the minimum electrical power normally required in a 24-hour period, which usually occurs over a time span at night. Strategies to reduce energy consumption at night are important in an economy very dependent on solar energy, in particular, photovoltaic.

## Population

13. That the national governments of each country having an ecological footprint in excess of its biocapacity create a population policy that would halt population growth and bring about a slow decline. Any such policy needs to have a large measure of public acceptance before it becomes effective.

# Appendix 1

## The Earth and Its Climate

Climate change is the greatest threat to life in general and the human race in particular, and is thus the prime reason for this book. So let's look at the Earth's climate, with a quick glance at its history, and try to understand why specific action is urgently needed.

For hundreds of millions of years, Earth has had a relatively stable climate in one of two modes: the warm ages, in which there were no ice caps at the poles; and the cool ages, with ice caps. About 252 million years ago, Earth was in a cool age, called the Permian, but a succession of natural causes put a tremendous volume of greenhouse gases into the atmosphere, driving the climate into a warm age, known as the Triassic, without ice caps. See A climate transition, below.

A greenhouse gas (ghg) is one that absorbs infrared radiation emitted from the Earth's surface, thus preventing some of that radiation from reaching outer space. It thus traps heat that, had it escaped, would have left the average surface temperature roughly constant.

For well over a million years, the Earth has been in a cold age, including numerous ice ages within the overall cool climate. And then, about 200 years ago, humanity started to put large amounts of carbon dioxide ($CO_2$) into the atmosphere. Initially it came from factories burning coal, and from domestic hearths, trains and steamships but, during the 20th century, it became the oil rush, with oil, natural gas and coal contributing to the total. The primary greenhouse gas is therefore $CO_2$, though other gases are also important, for example methane (when it escapes the Earth's surface unburned) and the oxides of nitrogen (mainly $N_2O$), which are formed when carbon fuels are burned in air at high temperatures.

The Earth's reaction is moderately fast on a geological timescale but, when we observe it on our human timescale, we can easily fail to come to grips with long-seeming delayed effects.

Putting a few thousand megatonnes of $CO_2$ into the atmosphere has, of itself, a modest enough effect on the balance between energy reaching the Earth's surface and the heat radiated back into space, but the delayed or continuing effects can go on for centuries. One continuing effect is the melting of glaciers and ice sheets. These reflect a great deal of the sunlight incident upon them, which is what keeps the Earth cool in an ice age. Once the ice is gone, the sunlight is strongly absorbed by land or water. Delayed processes include the emission of methane when the Arctic warms. The methane can come from the seabed or the tundra. Processes of this sort are called *feedbacks*, since they are not the primary causes of warming, but are triggered at different points during the warming. When a feedback adds to the warming, it is termed a positive feedback—though the effect may be very negative from a human standpoint! When a feedback counters the warming, as is the case when the added $CO_2$ increases photosynthesis, it is termed negative feedback. Most climate feedbacks are positive, which adds to the risk of a climate transition. A question then arises: by how much will the feedbacks, given enough time, multiply the warming directly due to the $CO_2$ emissions? Another unanswered question is: how long will it take for the feedbacks to produce their full effect?

Climate science has made great progress in identifying and estimating the effects of feedbacks, though the maximum total effect cannot yet be predicted with any precision. The reports from scientists working in the Arctic in recent years leave no doubt that positive feedback mechanisms are already at work there, but do not answer the question of increases to be expected in the global average temperature.

What this appendix presents, in fig.1.1, is the global average surface temperature increase since 1900 versus the natural logarithm of the $CO_2$ spanning the last 120 years. In fig.1.1 the temperatures are averaged over groups of up to ten successive years, to reduce the huge fluctuations in year-by-year data.

# CO$_2$ CONCENTRATION (ppm)

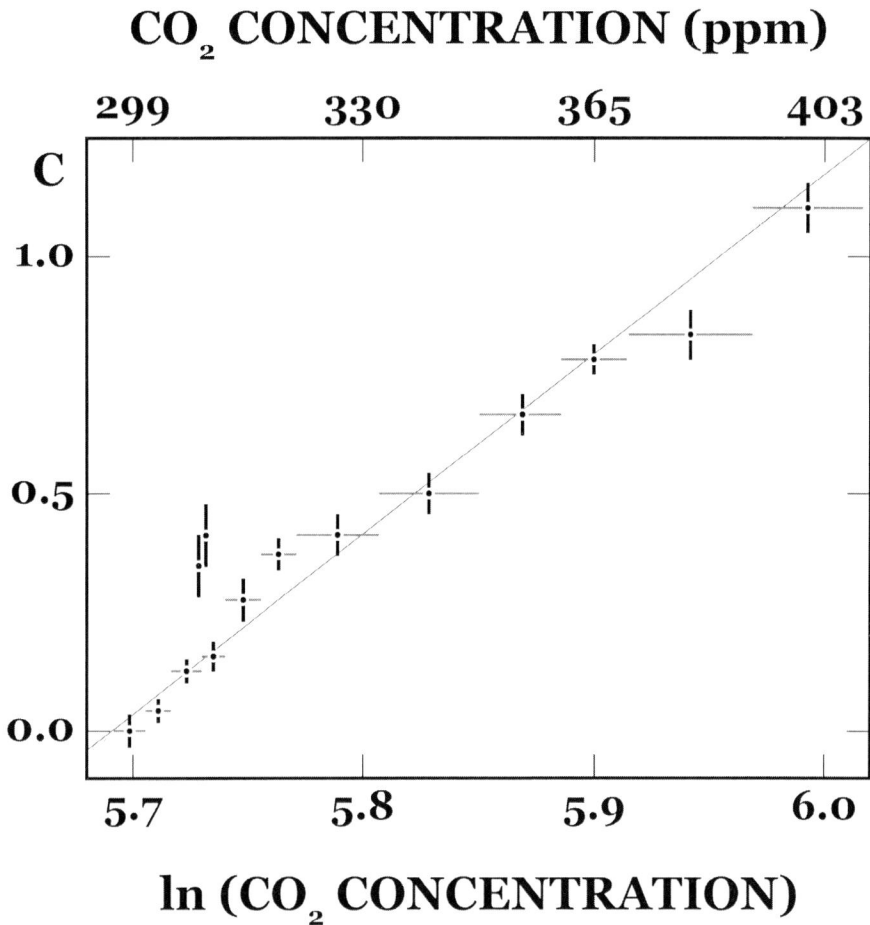

## ln (CO$_2$ CONCENTRATION)

Fig.1.1. The global average temperature increase since the reference period 1850-1900 is plotted versus the natural logarithm of the carbon dioxide concentration measured in parts per million (ppm). Even after the averaging over ranges of concentration, the data display considerable deviations from the straight line, but the linear relationship is at least approximately correct, with the exception of two very high points near the bottom left. The data for the temperature were taken from the NASA Goddard Institute for Space Studies [1], and the data on carbon concentrations are from BerkeleyEarth [2].

A few additional comments on fig.1.1 are necessary. The vertical bars for each point indicate the statistical uncertainties in the temperature. The higher of the two high points, near the bottom left, has been claimed to arise from a global heating due to an extended El Niño event from 1939-42, but the finding is controversial and is not treated as certain here, except to say there was an El Niño event part of 1940 and much of 1941. The lower of the two high points comes from data for the years after the El Niño event (1942-46) and is unexplained. There is no simple formula for correcting for the effect of global average heating by El Niño, nor for correcting for global heating or cooling due indirectly to maxima and minima in solar flares. Thus the temperature data have to be taken as they are, except that I reduced the weighting of the two high points in fitting the data to the best straight line.

## Methane in the atmosphere since 1900

The atmosphere contains a tiny fraction of methane, which is about 25 times as effective as $CO_2$ (per molecule) in raising the global average temperature. The atmosphere's methane content had risen smoothly along with the $CO_2$ for many years prior to 2000, after which the methane level remained constant until 2007 and then resumed its upward trend. The halt in the increase in atmospheric methane does not mean there were no methane emissions during those seven years, but that the emissions were balanced by the slow conversion of atmospheric methane to $CO_2$. Reports coming from scientists engaged in Arctic research since 2009 have emphasized important emissions and potential emissions of methane from newly unfrozen tundra and from the ocean itself. The resumption of the increase of atmospheric methane from 2007 fits this picture. The contribution of methane to the warming rose from about 7 percent of the total in 1900 to 13 percent in 2018. Readers should be aware that methane data have tended to be published without estimates of the considerable uncertainties in the data.

## Climate sensitivity

An expression often heard in discussions of climate change is *climate sensitivity*. Its meaning is the global temperature rise expected by the time the $CO_2$ atmospheric content has risen to 560 ppm, double the level at the beginning of the industrial revolution. Extrapolating the fitted line in fig.1.1 leads to a climate sensitivity of 2 C, with a statistical uncertainty of at least 10 percent. A considerable increase in atmospheric methane would increase climate sensitivity.

## A climate transition

Why is a transition from a generally cool age to a generally warm age, without ice caps, to be avoided? We have only one answer: that the transition of 252 million years ago, "The Permian-Triassic," caused the greatest extinction of species in Earth's records. It resembles the transition the human race is currently setting in motion, in that its ghg emissions (which back then came from natural causes) were of the same sort of magnitudes as ours, though building more gradually.

A result of greatly increased carbon dioxide in the atmosphere is its diffusion into the ocean, creating carbonic acid. The extinctions must have arisen as the ocean became acidic to the point it stopped producing oxygen, and this killed off most of the marine life. Much plant life, including trees, also disappeared during the Permian-Triassic transition. The cause of the extinctions can today be stated with reasonable certainty. The direct cause was large-scale emission of hydrogen sulfide from the ocean, the chemistry having begun once the ocean, already acid, was depleted of oxygen. The production of large quantities of hydrogen sulfide was assisted by the abundant presence of phosphorus [3]. Today's ocean is in a state for a repetition of the Permian experience.

> Life on land depends on a living ocean.

So it is not the warming itself that will kill off mammal life and much else, but the near-death of the ocean. Acidification of the ocean is something the climate deniers cannot refute. The ocean has already become significantly less alkaline because of its absorption of $CO_2$, a process that urgently needs to be halted. And very many ocean species have become extinct since the industrial revolution began, many times the natural rate for such extinctions. In 2017, it was announced that Australia's Barrier Reef was dying, an appalling tragedy in the making. Meanwhile the acidification is accelerating, while the ghg emissions globally are still on the increase.

Eliminating emissions is a matter of survival, not economic convenience!

## A point of no return?

There is a point in global warming at which the feedbacks can continue the warming without the help of emissions produced by humankind. We are uncomfortably close to such a point, which, at all costs is to be avoided.

## Conclusion

We are facing a climate emergency. To address it, greenhouse gas emissions from burning fossil fuels must be reduced to near-zero in the shortest practicable time. This alone will not suffice; it will also be necessary to reduce the overall concentration of $CO_2$ in the atmosphere, which is already too high, and this will require sequestration.

## Notes

1. http://data.giss.nasa.gov/gistemp/graphs/

2. http://sealevel.info/co2_and_ch4.html

3. Paul Werbos, private communication, June 2021. Peter Ward *A New History of Life* chapter 12 Bloomsbury Publishing 2016.

# Appendix 2
## Important projections

Chapter One and Appendix 1 have, I hope, convinced some readers that we really don't have much time to put things right when it comes to climate change. And the task is huge. Therefore, anything that diverts or delays human attention from this task could be fatal in the long term. The collapse of civilization is an immediate global example, since the institutions and governance of civilization will be needed for the huge collective effort of humans to address the climate threat.

### The collapse of civilizations

In his book *The Collapse of Complex Societies* (1988), Joseph Tainter tells us not only about the reasons for collapse of past civilizations, but also of identifiable stages in the process. In Jared Diamond's work, *Collapse* (2005), he examines the process in various states and empires, and includes examples of a few island societies that managed to avoid collapse. Ronald Wright, in *A Brief History of Progress* (2004) pegs his accounts of collapse on three phrases borrowed from Tainter, which describe two conditions leading to collapse and finally the collapse itself. These are the *runaway train*, the *dinosaur factor*; and the *house of cards*. Wright sees the runaway train of our own civilization as being due to population increase, the acceleration of technology, the concentration of wealth and power, and the *hemorrhage* of waste. Somehow the depleting capital resources got left out, but they are implicit, and he is stating that, with ruling power concentrated in too few hands, you can't enact a new system that would protect natural resources.

The dinosaur factor today is obvious: crucially important national leaders and other influential people not recognizing that we are following typical behavior of past failed civilizations.

The house of cards, the collapse itself, cannot be predicted, but one of the useful indicators is likely to be the state of the world's forests, since our woods are the keepers of water, and past civilizations that failed to preserve their forests collapsed, so we shall look briefly at the prospects for forest, globally.

## Three Projections

To provide a timescale for the kind of urgency we face, three projections are presented here, all relevant to the 21st century and the period within which we must regulate our behavior *vis-à-vis* ghg emissions and climate change in general. The first two resulted from the use of a computer modeling tool, the Global Systems Simulator (GSS), which integrates economic stocks and throughput globally. It was developed by Robert Hoffman, a professional economist who ran a modeling business in Ottawa. He was also, in his latter years, a member of the Club of Rome. He and his colleagues made the GSS available to the Global Issues Project (GIP) [1] at two international roundtables to demonstrate projection of scarcities, with the following results:

1) Forests. Under assumptions of *laissez-faire*, which means free-market attitudes and economic practices at the time of these studies (2006-2009), a severe *tension* will arise in the world's forest sector by the year 2038, meaning that supply will fall far short of demand. There'll be a marked shortage of lumber. Only immature, small-diameter trees will be available worldwide. Such a situation will have arisen because of overcutting, illegal cutting and deliberate burning of forest over many decades, all of which were continuing as I wrote in 2021 [2]. The plundering of tropical rainforests in some countries has been known for many years, notwithstanding persistent international efforts to conserve these vital resources. The effects of excessive harvesting can be seen in many other places. The GIP used Hoffman's GSS twice, well separated in years, to look at the forest sector, obtaining the date 2038 for the tension onset both times—see fig. 2.1. The results suggest a widespread lack of awareness of the dangers of

losing forest. Cutting, worldwide, legal and illegal, follows demand and far exceeds what is sustainable. Overcutting is thus widespread, though some jurisdictions manage to limit cutting to sustainable levels within their boundaries.

## WOOD TENSION

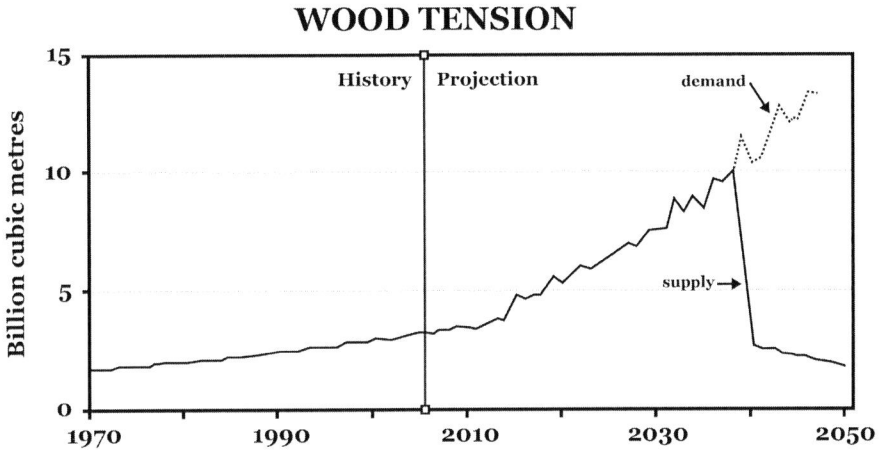

Fig. 2.1 Modeling result for supply and demand of lumber from about 1970 to 2050, under *laissez-faire*. Until 2038, supply meets demand every year. In 2038 the supply drops drastically creating a huge gap (tension) between demand and supply. If we suppose instead that the coming tension is anticipated and addressed, say, around 2025, then the wood tension begins much earlier but is less severe, and the decline now to be expected in 2038 becomes slight and leads to a more ample supply from 2050 on. The rising demand curve beyond 2038 is a feature of the model that would not be reproduced in the lumber trade, since substitutes for wood products would be sought.

2) We also used the GSS in 2009 to assess world population, for which the model requires current population figures, average birth rates, death rates, information on agriculture (available land for agriculture and its fertility), and any other relevant inputs. The model then projects the future food output and global population, which can indicate widespread food sufficiency or famine. Given a complete set of inputs, and again

assuming economic *laissez-faire*, we arrived at an age of global food tension by about the year 2040, with population peaking between 2040 and 2050. The onset of the decline is attributed to famine. An early, voluntary cessation of global population growth could enable the world to avoid the horrific threat of widespread famine. While no major reduction of the large annual growth in population has been seen as yet, it is worth noting that a slow reduction of the annual population increases began in 2013 and continued progressively to 2021, which is at least a good sign.

Lastly there's the work of twelve oceanographers [3], who estimate the end of commercial fishing of wild ocean fish by 2048, by which time they projected there would be too few fish of any size to make it worthwhile for any fishing boat to set out to sea. In the meantime, there will be an increase in fish farming, but we have no way of attempting to predict its output.

Joel Bourne Jr, however, has published an important and thorough study of food production and its likely future trends, *The End of Plenty* (2015). This work faces up to the probable nine billion people to be fed in the 2040s. Though Bourne admits some pessimism, he sees a few possibilities for an increase in food production. Fish farming, especially, may be entering a new age for production without ocean pollution.

To conclude these dreary projections, the human race can only expect horrendous shortages and their social consequences under *laissez-faire*, and the projected dates for these immense *tensions*, when last examined, lay between 2038 and 2048.

Evidently, *laissez-faire* isn't good enough.


**Notes**

1. The Global Issues Project, founded in Toronto, Ontario, was run by small *ad hoc* group that planned and cohosted seven international roundtables on crucial world issues, 2006-2012, each time with well-known cosponsoring partners.

2.    Today (2023) it would seem that deliberate burning has been replaced by forest fires becoming frequent because of conditions arising from global warming.

3. B Worm et al. "Impacts of biodiversity loss on ecosystem services" *Science* **314** (2006) pp. 9884-9888.

# Appendix 3
## Ecological Footprint

Studies in ecological footprint and biocapacity investigate the question: can the land and waters of a given country sustain the human population and absorb the pollution produced by human activities? By quantifying both footprint and biocapacity the Global Footprint Network provides valuable information on these matters, online [1].

The concept of footprint is so important that readers unfamiliar with it will need to understand it. It was introduced in 1992 by Bill Rees, a professor since retired from the University of British Columbia [2]. He was joined by a graduate student, Mathis Wackernagel, and together they explored the concept and refined it [3]. Today (2023), Wackernagel is President of the Global Footprint Network with its head office in Oakland [4].

During the past 20 years, the evaluation of footprint has become increasingly sophisticated and accurate. Along with the study of footprint (the impact humanity has on its territory and waters) they evaluate *biocapacity*—the ability of land and waters to supply human needs and absorb human pollution. Both the footprint and the biocapacity of a nation can be expressed as areas, the biocapacity being what one has to sustain life, while the footprint is what one would need to have to live in the same style sustainably. If the footprint exceeds the biocapacity, that society is living beyond its ecological means, either by extravagance or through polluting excessively. If the footprint is smaller than the biocapacity, all is well, at least for now.

There can be slight confusion here as footprint is often referred to as the ratio of the two areas, while immediately above it is defined as an area. Perhaps the ratio should be called specific footprint, or sustainability indicator, without dimensions.

The Global Footprint Network's emails provide the following vital information very nicely. First, they tell us how the world is doing ecologically, as a whole and also nation by nation. Second, they tell us what kinds of activities are contributing to the footprint sector by economic sector, so that ministries, municipalities, other authorities, corporations, businesses, institutions and individuals can take appropriate action. Third, they tell us the aggregate global footprint went into the overshoot mode (footprint exceeding biocapacity) c.1969, and that the excess has continued to increase since then. We are using resources future generations will need, and/or we are polluting the Earth system more and more.

Wackernagel and Beyers' book [5] is strongly recommended, especially for its emphasis on biocapacity and diagrams illustrating how the world and how individual nations overstepped the sustainable limit and went into "overshoot mode," and for its chapter on footprint and city planning. Their layer-cake diagrams show how different sectors of the economy contribute to the footprint. In many countries the portion of greenhouse gas emissions coming from fossil fuels contributes nearly half the footprint. For some prosperous countries, the footprints (in 2019) amounted to about 2.7 times what is sustainable. This means that, in such countries, even after eliminating fossil-fuel burning, overall consumption will have to be reduced considerably.

## Notes

1. footprints@footprintnetwork.org

2. Rees, William E (October 1992) "Ecological footprints and appropriated carrying capacity: what urban economics leaves out" *Environment and Urbanization*
    4 (2): 121–130.doi:10.1177/095624789200400212

3. Wackernagel, Mathis and William Rees *Our Ecological Footprint* New Society Press 1996.

4. Global Footprint Network · 312 Clay Street, Suite 300 · Oakland, CA 94607-3510 · USA

5. Mathis Wackernagel and Bert Beyers *Ecological Footprint: Managing Our Biocapacity Budget* New Society Publishers 2019.

# Appendix 4

## Biochar and Climate Change

Farmers and gardeners worldwide have recognized that biochar increases the fertility of soils, and it is being used in varying degrees on all continents. Biochar also has other uses. Its production has taken off in at least 32 countries, and that number is growing. The International Biochar Initiative in 2018 listed 62 companies that produce biochar and another 82 that produce equipment to produce biochar. The delivered cost of biochar is high for large-scale usage in agriculture; growers are therefore finding ways to use small amounts of biochar effectively. Biochar of the best quality remains active for very many years, so a reasonable policy could include its subsidy to enable farmers to attain organic status in a minimum time.

Biochar enthusiasts have long maintained that it will greatly assist in addressing climate change as plants grown in biochar-treated soil naturally sequester carbon dioxide [1]. While the potential for additional sequestration is considerable, the benefit of using biochar has a cost, namely, that carbon dioxide is emitted when the biochar is produced. Biochar is made by heating organic matter in a closed air-tight oven, but there's enough oxygen within the organic matter to produce about as many $CO_2$ molecules as there are carbon atoms left in the biochar. The question then is, which wins in the long term? The answer is "sequestration," but there is an interval of years before the quantity of $CO_2$ emitted is recovered, and the duration of that interval goes inversely as the difference in fertility gain by putting biochar into the soil. Thus, biochar as a means of sequestration works best in principle if very infertile land is made fertile [2]! And this will occur when the infertile soil has fertile matter added, other than biochar only, which again makes it difficult to separate the effect of the biochar from that of the other added ingredients.

The biochar story is, however, still incomplete. What might have been done with the materials from which the biochar is made, had they not been used to produce biochar? Had they been composted, there would have been greenhouse gases emitted during composting. Thus, producing biochar results in net emissions lower than those from the production alone.

Such considerations and much else, including cover crops and "inoculation" of biochar, are discussed by Jeff Cox, who guides the gardener toward optimal plant growth and health [3].

**Notes**

1. Dominic Woolf, James Amonette, Alayne Street-Perrot, Joseph Lehmann and Stephen Joseph "Sustainable Biochar to Mitigate Global Climate Change" *Nature Communications* **1** article 56 2010.

2. Derek Paul "Biochar-enhanced Sequestration of Atmospheric Carbon Dioxide" presented at the September 2010 Roundtable on Biochar in Toronto and published in *The Bulletin* of Science for Peace October 2010. www.scienceforpeace.ca

3. Jeff Cox *Gardening with Biochar* Storey Publishing 2019.

# Appendix 5
## Threats of Extinction of Wild Life

The story of the extinctions of wild life resulting from human folly or negligence is long, sad, and already old. The story continues, but much more starkly now, through the shrinking of habitat, due to developments arising from the huge numbers of people in almost all habitable areas of the planet—overpopulation. Human expansion began long ago, but on a small enough scale that it was easy to ignore until the years post WWII.

While human overpopulation is a major cause for concern, extinctions caused by human thoughtlessness and worse, deliberate slaughter, continue. Purposeless slaughter arises from failure to understand our proper relationship with the biosphere. The aboriginal people of North America never killed animals unnecessarily. They had learned through the experience of thousands of years that all were interdependent.

The 19th century exterminations are legion. They include the great awk, which was willfully exterminated by sailors for no reason other than their perverse pleasure. In 1800 the passenger pigeon throve in millions, but they were found to be good to eat, and their numbers declined, especially rapidly between 1870 and 1890, until the species was clearly threatened. The slaughter nevertheless continued until the last individual died in a zoo in 1914. Mammals are prominent in the long list of exterminations. Somehow, a few plains bison got preserved following willful destruction of millions of them in the 19th century. Of the bison family in North America today, only the wood bison have their own, protected territory and can live in the wild. The determination to kill for sport continues, with immense pressure on governments to allow killing of wolves where they exist in the wild. An approximation to the truth for surviving species in 2017 is that all wild mammals are threatened with extinction, for environmental reasons including loss of habitat, or because they are hunted for trophies, as is the case for tigers, elephants and rhinoceros, or for fun, or a combination of the foregoing.

Birds have declined tremendously in numbers this last half century, from loss of habitat and several other human-related causes. These latter include chemical pollution and deaths from cutting of forest during the nesting season. Smaller birds suffer tremendous losses from domestic cats, and significant losses in collisions with tall buildings and modern windmills, all of which are, in principle, preventable. The enormous annual loss of birds due to domestic cats increases with increasing human population. Tall buildings, likewise, are a result of human overpopulation.

Species in the ocean are no less under threat. First it was whales, then cod, now sharks and all other species, especially if edible. Trawling in the ocean increases the efficiency of the catch and proportionally the rate of loss of numbers remaining in the ocean, which can lead to extinction. There are UN mechanisms to help stop the decline, which are not yet sufficiently effective.

In the ocean also, huge numbers of species become extinct when a coral reef dies. Such reefs die from pollution, accelerated by ocean warming and decreasing alkalinity of the water. Avoiding further loss of alkalinity is hugely important for preserving life in the ocean—a prime reason that fossil fuels should no longer be burned. The state of the world's remaining coral is a sensitive measure of human destruction of the ecosphere. It became known in 2017 that the famous and wonderful Australian Great Barrier Reef is dying.

The Living Planet Index established that, on average, species declined in their numbers by 25 percent from 1970 to 2000 (Jonathan Loh et al. 2005 DOI:10.1098/rsto.2004.1584). Assuming an exponential decay, this represents almost 1.2 percent decline per year.

There was some good news on the animal front in 2022, including a reversal of the wild tiger decline, an end to Hong Kong's ivory trade, increases in the elephant population in Gabon and the giraffe population in Africa, and several more good news stories from other countries.

# Afterword

Readers of this book may have noticed the absence of text on the importance of potable water in all habitable regions of the world. Potable water is, however, a prime factor that makes a region habitable. Ensuring an adequate supply of freshwater for any growing population is an inescapable task. The omission of the topic in this book was deliberate, since questions of water supply for any growing population necessarily had to be addressed through the traditional economy, the subject being so important.

Marq de Villiers' book, *Water*, published by Stoddart Publishing in 1999, pays attention to human water requirements across the Globe and, in some detail, how these requirements were being met.

Fresh water can be taken from lakes and rivers, from underground aquifers, directly by collecting rainwater and by desalinating sea water, all of which are practised. Today, freshwater could also be collected from melting ice in the Arctic. So far, water has mainly been taken from lakes, rivers and aquifers, though pollution of rivers and lakes has been a major problem, and aquifers too can become polluted, especially if water is removed from them at too great rates. The removal of water from aquifers at rates greater than those at which nature will refill them usually leads to disaster, including the partial or total collapse of the aquifer itself. In the past, therefore, desperation to have an adequate sources of water for any population—and most populations are growing—has produced some very negative results in many countries.

Price has also entered strongly into the matter of water supplies. I had at one time felt that $4 (USD) per cubic m, that is, 0.4 cents/l, of fresh, potable water, was a reasonable price to pay for this essential substance, but those who have been in the business of supplying potable water or water for irrigation were usually looking for prices considerably lower than a tenth of my $4/m$^3$.

Villiers refers often enough to the growing population of a given country, where the water supply is modest, as being a serious concern, though he doesn't take sides with the writers and researchers who see the continually growing population as leading inevitably to collapse, or with those who take the opposite view, that problems of sufficiency and quality of water can be solved through ingenuity.

I must also mention the international competition for water resources, such as exist when a major river flows through several countries, each of which makes claims on their share of the water, often an inflated share! Many examples exist in which the sum of claims is greater than the total water available, and such struggles between nations are not often settled quickly, and can lead to violence, even war, if a country withholding water leads to desperation within the neighbor country. The division of rights to water is not limited to rivers, and applies to any source of water that is to be shared.

De Villiers saw the entire global water problem as worsening with time, because all or nearly all populations were growing, and the water supplies were constant or diminishing, but he took some comfort from the slowing rates of population growth.

In the near future all aspects of water supply are likely to be more difficult and costly than was the case in the late 20th century. An ecological approach will be needed, and huge financial support is likely to be necessary and, even then, funding large-scale irrigation could require a new break-through in water purification methods. The ecological economy might include prevention of loss of the few remaining usable aquifers (if any!); but the human race will have to cope with a new distribution of water resources at higher prices. Investing in sustainable solutions as soon as possible is surely playing safe in this difficult matter of assuring adequacy of water supplies. Water sharing also calls for negotiation with understanding.

Preventing pollution of lakes and rivers will be increasingly important, in fact, essential, and the lessons of chapter 16, herein, may at last be put into practice.

**New construction of coal-burning power stations in China**

As this book was entering its production at the publishers, China announced that it planned to build many more coal-burning power plants to satisfy new demands for electricity. Quebec's leading newspaper, Le Devoir, put the case as follows on 28 February 2023, and I translate: the giant of Asia started in 2022 to construct coal-burning power plant six times better than any in the rest of the world… In all, projects totalling 106 GW output were approved in 2022.

This enormous increase in coal-burning electrical output is so stunning as to raise questions on the increasing likelihood of a climate disaster. We know nothing as yet, however, of possible Chinese intentions to use carbon capture and storage or to close down older coal-burning plant that has been highly polluting. It is therefore too early to speculate on the changes this new development might have on China's total ghg emissions.

**Last-minute news**

In his first public engagement following his coronation in May 2023, King Charles III of the UK broke ground for Cambridge University's new Whittle Laboratory. This multimillion facility will be the world's leading "disruptive innovation" laboratory for net-zero aviation and energy. [The added quotation marks are the author's.]

**About the author**: Derek Paul is a retired physicist, turned generalist. He obtained his Bachelor's degree from Cambridge University and then worked for three years in industry. In 1953 he took up residence in Kingston, Ontario teaching and doing research in atomic physics for a decade at the Royal Military College of Canada. He obtained a doctorate from Queens University in 1958. From 1964-95 he was a professor at the University of Toronto. In 1976 he became a participant in the Pugwash Conferences on Science and World Affairs, with their strong focus on peace issues. The Soviet invasion of Afghanistan in December 1979 and the maximum tension in the Cold War greatly changed his off-duty activities, which came to include co-founding Science for Peace (1981- ) and making several visits to the Soviet Union and one to East Germany, all by invitation. In the late 1990s he was a member of the new International Society for Quality of Life Studies. In 2005, he cofounded the Global Issues Project, which grew to a committee of eleven and organized international roundtables over seven years on crucial issues spanning forests, climate change, fresh water, food, population, a no-growth economy, biochar, and peace in outer space. He was motivated to write this book because of the urgent need to address the huge threat of climate change, reduce ecological footprint and increase biocapacity everywhere. He is a member of two physical societies, the International Society for Ecological Economics, Coalition Climat Montreal, the Canadian Association of the Club of Rome, and the Rassemblement des universitaires. He lives in Montreal.

# The Book Cover

The cover of this book is the reproduction of an oil painting by the author. It is a metaphor for the book itself, namely, the transition from the known to the unknown, since nothing quite like an ecological economy has been tried out these last 300 years except on a local scale. The young ballerina in the picture, c. 1978, shoeless, wearing her school uniform and protected from the rain by an umbrella as she flies through the air, has already started the descent from her *grand jeté.* Her flight toward greener pastures can also be interpreted as a metaphor for the better human society that will result from a dynamic ecological economy. She cannot know exactly what the terrain will be like when she lands (another piece of the metaphor), but land she must, and the rain adds to the uncertainty.

[The dancer is not related to the author]

# Index

168

169